Lineage

Also by Robert Root

MEMOIR

Happenstance

ESSAY COLLECTIONS

Postscripts: Retrospections on Time and Place
Limited Sight Distance: Essays for Airwaves

NONFICTION OF PLACE

Recovering Ruth: A Biographer's Tale
Following Isabella: Travels in Colorado Then and Now
Walking Home Ground: In the Footsteps of Muir, Leopold &
Derleth

ANTHOLOGIES

Working at Writing: Columnists and Critics Composing
Landscapes with Figures: The Nonfiction of Place
The Island Within Us: Isle Royale Artists-in-Residence 1991-1998
(with Jill Burkland).
The Fourth Genre: Contemporary Writers of/on Creative
Nonfiction
(with Michael Steinberg)
Those Who Do, Can: Teachers Writing, Writers Teaching
(with Michael Steinberg)

LITERARY STUDIES

E. B. White: The Emergence of an Essayist
The Nonfictionist's Guide: On Reading and Writing Creative
Nonfiction

LINEAGE

Reading the Past to Reach the Present

Robert Root

The Humble Essayist Press

The Humble Essayist Press
Blairsville, Georgia 2020

To those who came before
and those came—and will come—after

Lineage

Contents

They were on to something, Zee thought.
We aren't haunted by the dead,
but by the impossible reach of history.
By how unknowable those others are to us,
how unfathomable we'd be to them.

(Rebecca Makkai, *The Hundred-Year House*)

When all those who knew you as a child are dead,
what happens to your history,
to all those lives you lived?

(Rebecca McClanahan, *The Tribal Knot*)

PRELUDE

The photo app on my cellphone has well over two thousand photographs and videos stored on it; the iPhoto app on my laptop has all of them and everything from the cellphone before this one, images going back nearly a dozen years. Note the language I'm using here: I don't believe I've ever written the word "app" before and have seldom spoken it, and my using the words "cellphone" and "laptop" together with "app" speak to the technological age in which I write this (on my laptop computer, which has actually never been on my lap). All of those images are also preserved in the "iCloud," wherever that is, and possibly on a back-up hard drive I sometimes remember to connect to my computer. My son, who is more hip to technology than I could ever be, tells me that in the near future further changes will come to the systems I'm familiar with—CDs, I've learned, are on the way out, though like vinyl recordings now reappearing, may one day be revived by nostalgic troglodytes of former generations—and I recall the transformations information-storage has undergone since I first encountered computers: floppy disks replaced by hard discs and then flash drives, and videotapes supplanted by DVDs. I think how proud my brother and his wife were to have "uploaded" all their family photos and videotapes to computer disks some years ago and how dismayed my wife has been to realize her new computer lacks certain ports and relies only on wireless connections. I think of the slides in the box in my garage that I never view for lack of a slide projector—my brother uploaded his long ago. I think of my collection of 45s, EPs, and LPs moldering in storage. I think of boxes with my mother's scrapbooks and photo albums, my father's memorabilia.

I seem to have a penchant for preservation, for collection and storage, but only now, in the era in which I am too aware of my age and of the complications of access to what I've collected and stored, am I wondering whether preservation is really possible. More urgently, I wonder what I might learn from what I've preserved before I run out of time to learn it. The swift passage of time, which seems ever swifter to me these days, keeps nudging me to look into the past, to consider what's irretrievable and what of the previously

1

unknown might be deciphered somehow. I ponder old photographs, read old notes and letters, gaze into the faces of my ancestors, and try to interpret—to read—what I consider to be their literary remains. I want to make a stab at preserving who they were, even if all I'm preserving is best guesses at who they were. I also wonder if reading their words and pondering their images—investigating such evidence of my lineage as I can find—will tell me something about who I am.

ANCESTRY

LINEAGE

An optimist would say that each of us comes from a long line of survivors. Think of all the circumstances over the millennia that have decimated, obliterated, or exterminated family lines: war, plague, cataclysm, disease, genocide, homicide, suicide, accident, mere infertility; think of the circumstances that continue to terminate them, the numbers of the dead in the first two decades of the twenty-first century alone, the lives and lineages that have been cut off by deliberate devastation or natural disaster. If you think of all that, you have to marvel, if only for a moment, that all *your* ancestors made it through, passed on their essences this far—as far, that is, as *you*. Some would say that we—you the reader, I the writer, and everyone else we see around us every day—have somehow been selected to be here. Whether you think that it was inevitable or inadvertent, that you were somehow *meant* to be here or that you simply blundered into existence, it would be sensible, considering the alternatives, to feel both gratitude and relief. So too you might be curious about the course of ancestral descent that got you here.

Happily enough, curiosity about the past is widespread, especially about questions of lineage. Anytime I'm in a historical library, genealogical archive, or family history center, I find myself among numerous, intense others thumbing through card catalogs, bending over old books, and squinting into microform readers. I've heard that, as a popular hobby, genealogy is second only to gardening. A staggering amount of public records and private documents has been preserved and disseminated over the years, and far-flung resources exist for the dogged and determined family researcher.

At the outset the task seems simple: you come from two people, and those two people themselves come from two people each. Your grandparents' generation is connected to four families. Then it gets complicated. Since each person in your family tree comes from two people who come in turn from four people, the branches multiply rapidly; if you could trace patrilineal and matrilineal lines for each individual, you would find yourself distantly related to a vast population. My father's father was a Root;

my father's mother was a Ross—two families. My grandfather's mother was a Donaldson; my grandmother's mother was a Lathrop—four families. On my grandfather's side of the family my search through earlier generations uncovers twelve more families, the ones that the wives of the Root and Donaldson men came from in those generations. This total passes over all the families of the mothers of the women who married Root men or all the families of the other wives of Root men who bore half-brothers and half-sisters of my progenitors. On my grandmother's side, in addition to the Rosses and Lathrops, I identify ten more families for certain; in sum, twenty-six families are directly linked to my father, who was in the tenth generation of Roots, the eleventh of Lathrops to live in America. For now, I'm mentioning only my father's family tree, holding off on my mother's side of the family—I could probably add an equal number of families to those already counted and have a total, more or less, of some fifty families in the same time span, even more if I investigate the European generations that preceded them.

To sort all these families out would be a daunting prospect for anyone compulsively compiling an absolutely accurate family tree—picture it spreading from you out across a space as large as a gymnasium floor. On the other hand, it should be a calming thought for anyone feeling isolated in life—the world is well populated with your relatives.

But if you aren't obsessive about lineage, your search is simpler and more readily achievable: you only have to find what you can about the family history of the four people who produced your two parents.

*   *   *

The population of North America is overwhelmingly composed of immigrants and their descendants. In theory, if not always in practice, every family can trace itself back to a pioneer generation, the first individuals in their line to transplant themselves from the old country to the new. Beyond the pioneer generations are likely to be generations harder to trace in countries of origin. For a great span of human history last names were specific to the individual, identifying only his or her parentage or occupation or domicile, and the surnames, particularly for the common folk, came later on.

James Pierce Root, in *Root Genealogical Records 1600-1870,* argues, after weighing and discarding a number of alternatives, that the most likely origin for the Root family name is that given in the *"Patronymica Brittanica,* a learned work by Lower": "Rootes—probably from Routes and Routtes, a commune in the arrondissement of Yvetot, in Normandy (Lower Seine)." The name then comes from a place and links us back to the Normans, who conquered England in 1066 and brought Norman names and French language to the island. Says Root: "The most reasonable theory yet suggested is that the name originally was spelt ROOTES, and was of two syllables, and has suffered the loss of the two final letters by contraction . . . as the members of the family have traveled northward in England, and westward in America."

The Lathrop name has undergone similar transformations from similar origins. The Rev. E. B. Huntington, a Lathrop descendent, in his *Genealogical Memoir of the Lo-Lathrop Family,* describes the origin in prose that sounds on the ear like a Monty Python sketch: "Lowthorpe is a small parish in the wapentake of Dickering, in the East Riding of York, four and a half miles northeast from Great Driffield, having about 150 inhabitants. It is a perpetual curacy in the archdeaconry of York. This parish gave name to the family of Lowthrop, Lothrop, or Lathrop." Huntington traces records of the family back to 1216, the year after King John signed the Magna Carta and the first year of the reign of nine-year old Henry III, when Walter de Lowthorpe was elected sheriff for Yorkshire. He also cites a record of Robert de Louthrop serving as a chaplain in St. Martin's Church in Lowthorpe during the reign of Richard the Second (1377-1399).

These are, admittedly, vague connections to my own existence, but as a former student of medieval English history and literature, even vague connections to the Norman Conquest, the King John of the Robin Hood era, and the Richard II of Shakespeare's play give me considerable pleasure.

On my mother's side of the family the names are more problematic, as they tend to be with ancestors from non-English speaking countries. The spellings of foreign names often get garbled in immigration records and eventually they reflect, if not the changes those agents have made, then the impact of American pronunciations. Linderman was once Lindemann and at least the spelling and pronunciation are close, but Stanley Budnack entered this country, very likely, as Stanislaw or Stanislaus Budniack or Burdnzak and his last name was rendered as Budnac or Budnick in official records. His wife, according to family lore, was Hedwig Leveque, though the official records name her Jaidwega (Hedwig was closer to the likely pronunciation) and never provide her maiden name.

Pronunciation is a minor factor, though it can affect how others record the spelling. I am forever spelling out my last name, even to florists, who seem unfamiliar with the word "root," and emphasizing the 't' to avoid being heard as "rude" or "ruth." We in my family pronounce Root to rhyme with "fruit" or "toot" or "loot" (and don't think we haven't heard people use those rhymes against us) while others pronounce it to rhyme with "put" or "foot." Even so, people often ignore one of the o's or think that the "oo" is always "u" and we get mail addressed to "Rot" or "Rut." Imagine what happens to names in a culture or country relying on oral transmission.

Genealogical research, I've come to learn, is a kind of cold case detective work that runs the gamut from overabundant evidence to unrewarding dead end. Luckily for me, three of the four families who produced my father's parents lived in America long enough, left enough records, and achieved sufficient prominence that the work of tracking them down has already been done for me. In the late nineteenth century, perhaps prompted by the nation's centennial and a wide-spread sense of national accomplishment, the origins and achievements of families, cities and towns, counties, and states were prolifically recorded and celebrated in collective histories and biographies of "eminent men" of one locale or another. For anyone of my generation descended from such families, it requires only being able to identify our great-grandparents to tie into histories extending back to colonial or post-Revolutionary days and often beyond.

At least two of those four families leading to my father are subjects of detailed genealogies stretching back over centuries. Such family histories trace predictable paths. Beginning with the effort to determine the origin of the family name, they try to locate the earliest ancestors documented in public records or private papers. They determine the identities of the first family members to migrate to North America and, as fully as possible, trace the lines of descent from them down to those descendants living at the time the genealogy was compiled. In most cases the authors are themselves descendants and relatives of the people documented in the history. The earlier the American portion of the histories begin, the more the family history parallels the history of the nation: the origins on the east coast, particularly New England; the involvement in settlement and resettlement and the early wars with Native Americans; the American Revolution; the movement westward as more of the country opened up to settlement after the Louisiana Purchase, the War of 1812, the opening of the Erie Canal, the Mexican War, the Gold Rush, and the Civil War; involvement in the civic life of the communities where the families often spent generations. Some portion of these families was always moving, picking up and pioneering onto a newer frontier, but another portion would remain where they started, developing ties to place and community. It is the happenstance of who moves on and who stays behind that determines who is in a certain locale when the time comes for them to find a marriage partner, have children, and continue the family lines. For my father's parents to meet, fall in love, and marry in Cooperstown, New York—and produce my father—generations of Roots and Donaldsons, Lathrops and Rosses had to make certain decisions about migration and settlement; for my mother's parents to meet, fall in love, and marry in Niagara County, New York—and produce my mother—only one generation of Lindermans and Budnacks had to make those decisions. The prime decision, of course, was to come to this country in the first place.

*   *   *

At the very least, lineage can tell you where you come from and how your parents happened to be who they were and how they happened to be where you were conceived. I use the word "happen" deliberately. If you want to believe that intention and design determined your creation, rather than happenstance, tracing your lineage will highlight how complicated the chain of events needed to be in order to result precisely in *you*.

Take, for example, if you were born an American, the circumstance that your progenitors came to this continent from somewhere else. At the close of the sixteenth century and the beginning of the seventeenth, all my ancestors were in Europe, my father's ancestors scattered around the British Isles, my mother's likely somewhere in central Europe. On both sides of my family I know when the last European-born generation arrived on these shores and when the first American-born generation was born. In some cases I know something of what brought the Europeans to America.

That's the other dimension to the lineage question. It isn't simply the facts that matter, interesting as they are—not merely names and dates and locations and chronologies—but also the motives, the activities, perhaps the personalities of your ancestors that are significant. The facts help determine matters of public record and biology (why you live in Western New York and have hazel eyes); the personalities help explain matters of private identity and psychology (why you work in education or the arts instead of in agriculture or industry). Unique and individual each of us may be but we all bear the influences of our upbringings, just as our parents, who shaped that upbringing, bore the influences of theirs, just as our grandparents did, and so on. It isn't necessarily a tightly predetermined chain, more like a series of merging or diverging rivulets flowing inevitably downhill from the massive snowpack of prehistory, but a good many of the connections or disconnections can be located.

So, in regard to lineage, there are two questions to answer: Who were the people you came from? How did who they were influence the kind of people your parents were? Expect to examine incomplete evidence as thoroughly as you can and eventually have to accept the need to settle for surmise.

PIONEERS

Having long ago studied literary figures of the seventeenth and eighteenth centuries, I'm familiar with the portraits of the long dead as captured by portraitists in paint and ink. But I've never known what to conclude about the character of the individuals in the portraits. What can you take on face value (literally) about the people you gaze upon? Is it possible to recover resemblance over eleven generations, between this man born at the end of the sixteenth century and my father, his descendent, born early in the twentieth century? I have been blithely content to only be able to identify my grandparents in photos taken when they were younger, but when I discover the picture of John Lothroppe in that genealogical history of the Lothrop-Lathrop family, I photocopy it, scan it into my computer, and occasionally enlarge it to the size of some family portraits, as if I hope to recognize him if we pass on some timeless street.

John Lothroppe is credited as the family pioneer, the head of the line from which, through my great-grandmother, Mary Lathrop Ross, I am descended, and the one who first emigrated from England to America. As it happens, he was something of a notable individual, which you need to be to have aspects of your life recorded in enough detail that they can be recovered centuries later.

I'm fascinated by the specificity of information that "genealogical memoir" provides for a man who lived four hundred years ago. Born in December 1584, John Lothroppe was one of eighteen children fathered by Thomas Lothroppe of Yorkshire, one of five birthed by Thomas's second wife, Mary. In 1609 he graduated with an M. A. from Queen's College, Cambridge, then served from around 1611 until 1623 as the curate of an Anglican parish church southeast of London, in Kent. One account of his life claims he "labored faithfully as long as his judgment could approve the ritual and government of the Church," but gave up his Anglican curacy to become the pastor of the First Independent Church in London. A congregation of dissenters, their worship services were illegal. Lothroppe led the congregation through eight years of secret meetings until, on 22 April 1632, he and forty-two other members were arrested and imprisoned. Two years later all but Lothroppe were released. He was allowed to visit his wife, the mother of his nine children, when she fell ill, but was returned to prison. After she died, his children won his release through the Anglican bishop and he was ordered to appear before King James I's Star Chamber. Instead, Lothroppe sailed to Massachusetts, his arrival noted by Governor John Winthrop in his journal entry for 18 September 1634: "Mr. Lathrop [actually Lothroppe] and Mr. Sims, two godly ministers coming in the same ship." Lothroppe joined members of his London congregation in Scituate, Massachusetts but soon relocated with some of them to Barnstable. He died there on 8 November 1653, credited by one biographer as "a good and true man, an independent thinker, and a man who held opinions in advance of his times." Clearly John Lothroppe made a good impression on a number of people.

I've found no corresponding image anywhere of John Roote, the pioneer in my particular line of the Root family, known in the genealogies as "the Farmington line," but he has a somewhat similar if less detailed story recorded about him. Born 26 February 1608, in Badby, Northamptonshire, England, the son of John and Mary (Russell) Root, it is said of him that he was orphaned and adopted by his father's brother. When civil war between the supporters of King Charles I and the supporters of Parliament grew imminent, John was supposedly urged by his adamantly anti-Royalist uncle to join the forces of Oliver Cromwell, but, because he "had an aversion to war," he instead joined a group of Puritans bound for the American colonies. It's unclear exactly when this took place, but he is counted among the first settlers of Farmington, Connecticut in 1640. Sometime around then he married Mary Kilbourne, who had come to the New World with her parents, Thomas and Mary Kilbourne, on the ship *Increase* in 1635. Their first child, the beginning of the American-born Farmington line, was born in 1642, three hundred years before I was born. Their third son, Thomas Roote, from whom I am directly descended (and of whom I had no knowledge when I named my son Thomas in 1973), was born in 1648.

The line of descent from John Lothroppe is somewhat less straightforward. Two of his English-born children, Thomas and Joseph, are important for the line that descends to my father, though the trail is a little complicated. Joseph Lothropp, born in 1624, likely came with his father to Massachusetts, and married Mary Ansell in 1650. The tenth of their twelve children was a son, Hope, born in 1671. Joseph's older brother Thomas, born in 1621, married Sarah Larned Ewer, a widow, in 1639. Their fourth child, Meletiah, born in 1646, married Sarah Farrar in 1667 and their daughter Elizabeth was born 15 November 1677. Here's where the complications come in: Hope Lothrop, Joseph's son and Thomas's nephew, married his second cousin Elizabeth Lathrop, Thomas's granddaughter, 15 November 1696, thus reuniting two branches of the Lathrop lineage. Hope Lothrop was the first American-born male on his side of that family intermarriage, and his wife's father the first American-born male on her side of the marriage. The emphasis on patrilineal rather than matrilineal descent gives the younger man precedence over his older cousin/father-in-law. I haven't figured out the genetic complications of this reconstituted family line.

These are facts of genealogy. They say relatively little about who these people were and other than tidbits of information in those family histories, it's hard to learn much more about them than names and dates.

And yet I wonder: knowing some anecdotal evidence about the decisions the man made, can we read anything of John Lothroppe's character in his portrait? Does he really seem intelligent, independent, thoughtful, earnest, or is that merely a projection of his resume onto his image? Is his piety and stubborn faith at all evident in his demeanor, the calm fixedness of his gaze, or is his gaze only an etcher's contribution or interpretation? Was

11

his Protestant faith the deciding element in the paths his descendants chose? As grandfather to the first two American-born patriarchs, what elements of his character might have been displayed in their demeanors? How is he different from John Roote (of whom I have no visual image), who arrived in America around the same time, not a minister of any faith but nonetheless in the company of Puritans and surely a man of similar resolution and drive? Here is one man who defied the Anglican Church and the Star Chamber of the King of England; here is another who chose emigration over rebellion.

The actions of these men determined that the future history of their descendants would be a colonial American history and ultimately a national American one. Is there any way to understand what those descendants inherited beyond location and circumstance? What comes down of character through the generations? How can it be traced? What impact does it have on those born centuries later, in generations almost unimaginably distant?

I return to John Lothroppe's portrait once more, enlarge it once more, wonder for once, if something about his eyes, about the set of his mouth, the shape of his jaw, are signs of his lineage in my father. Or in me. If John returned my gaze, would he almost recognize me?

FAMILY PORTRAIT ROSS

I have only a scanned-in copy of a reproduction of this photograph in my collection. I'd like to know the type of photograph—not a daguerreotype or ambrotype, probably, too late for that, perhaps a tintype or a photograph made by the time-consuming wet collodion process—but the pleasure for me is in having a copy of something so old. It's the earliest photo I have of any branch of my family tree, dated 1868, and as chance would have it is one of the photos I've most recently acquired. Until a few months ago I had no idea any of these people ever existed—that is, I knew of course that my antecedents had antecedents and that some such group as this must have produced one of my great-grandparents, but the names of this particular group were unknown to me. I had also never imagined I would get to see their faces.

Note the expressions on those faces, if you can. On my computer I've zoomed in again and again to enlarge their faces; happily, digital imaging keeps things clear and vivid, and I was able to have close up views of all of them. Of the eight people in the family portrait, only one, the father, has anything like a smile on his face. The rest of the family members have in common a tight-lipped, blank-faced, almost sullen expression. I attribute this to the circumstances of the photography, the need for everyone to sit absolutely still while the photograph is being taken, perhaps for minutes at a time, and fortunately I've seen enough historical portraits of this kind to avoid assuming that my ancestors were a grim and cheerless lot.

According to an inscription on the back of the photograph the people in the portrait are William and Flora Ross and their six children. Pictured from left to right are Chauncy, on the arm of the sofa; the semi-smiling bearded father William; Louise standing to his left; Anne, seated in front of her; Will, the youngest child; Clara, also standing; Flora, their mother, seated; and, holding up the end, the black clad eldest son, Charles. Despite the humorless expressions on their faces, the portrait suggests a close and affectionate family. Note how casually Will is leaning against the back rest between his oldest sisters, how Chauncy rests an arm on his father's shoulder, how William's left arm embraces his youngest daughter and how she nestles against him, how Charles leans on his mother's shoulder and stands semi-relaxed on one leg with the other crossed. Could the father's amused expression be pleasure in the company of his wife and children, the informality of the poses a reflection of family intimacy? Given no further evidence to contradict the image, I read it according to my inclinations.

As it happens, this family that I have a picture of is the family I knew least about of my father's ancestral lines. The others I can trace a long way back, but the Rosses stopped at my great-grandfather until this photo turned up and sent me searching through census records. William Ross, the father in the photo, is the family pioneer. He was born in Ireland in 1825, the son of Thomas Ross and Louise Campbell, undoubtedly a Scots-Irish couple. I don't know when he came to America but on 7 June 1852 he married Flora Ellison in Bridgeport, Connecticut. She was also born in Ireland, in 1827, the daughter of Charles and Margaret Ellison. The Reverend William Ross was a Methodist minister who shifted among congregations over the years. Their first child, Louise, was born in New York State, their second, Clarissa, in Massachusetts. Charles, their first son and the first American-born male of that line, was born in Stanwich, Connecticut, in 1855. The younger children, Chauncy, Anne, and William, were also born in Connecticut. As the photograph shows us, in 1868 the family was complete.

The photo makes them more real to me than the families I can trace back generation by generation to the late sixteenth and early seventeenth centuries. They make me realize that, in all the historical portraits I've seen, I've tended to remain aloof from the subjects. Since the poses were formal and constrained, mere shadings of black and white, in costumes and among furnishings that had no resonance for me, I tended not to interrogate the pictures. Whatever they were witness to in their lives, their families, their era, I can read little in their expressions that intimate what any of that might have been.

So it is with the family pictures I've been in over the decades. What an outsider sees or interprets is not what the inhabitants of a picture recognize, realize, remember when they see the photograph again. Just so, these people, most of whom lived long after the photograph was taken, must have viewed this picture later in life with all their accumulated experience altering their vision, their perception of what they behold. I know at least that my great-grandfather owned this picture until late in his life—how else would it have come to my cousin Janet except through her mother and our mutual grandmother and our great-grandfather? What did he make of the family he saw from the privileged perspective of age? What did he think of the boy in black leaning so nonchalantly on his mother's shoulder? What did he think of the man—the husband, father, businessman—the boy grew up to become or of the children he and his wife brought into the world or of the man (my grandfather) one of his daughters chose as her husband?

I haven't any answers to those questions but I believe he must have thought about these things as he viewed the family portrait. Before his own death, he'd lost both his parents and his brother Chauncy, but his three sisters were all married and his brother William still alive. Surely he had time to think about his losses and his gains over the years. The idea of him holding up the picture and reflecting upon the familiar faces and the life they had together makes me feel considerably less distant from this man I never knew and from this family and its eldest child, the boy he once was.

*   *   *

15

The formal photograph of Charles Wilbur Guyon Ross has the handwritten words "Father 1915" written across the bottom border. The handwriting is his daughter's, my grandmother's. The picture was taken three years before her wedding to my grandfather and five years before my great-grandfather's death, at age 64, in 1920. I'm happy to have a copy of the photograph, which passed from my grandmother to my aunt, my father's younger sister, and then to my cousin, Janet. Because I come so late to tracking this history down, Charles Ross is a surprise to me, another face I've never seen before, until recently, and another person I try to read on only the evidence of two photos.

Luckily, in the files of the New York State Historical Society in Cooperstown, I am able to find his obituary, which tells me some details about his life and his death. When he married Mary Lathrop in Cooperstown on August 12, 1890, he married into a well-established Cooperstown family; his wife was the granddaughter of a prominent lawyer and the daughter of a prominent doctor and those men could trace their descent back across time to that dissenting clergyman, John Lothroppe. The house in which the Rosses lived and where Charles died had been his father-in-law's house, where his wife had grown up and where my grandmother and her sisters also grew up. My grandmother was the only one of his daughters to marry and his only grandchild, her first child, Arthur Pier Root Jr., had been born only three weeks before Charles died. He had been in ill health for a couple of months before "a second paralytic shock . .

. after which his decline became rapid." His brother William and sisters Clara, Louise, and Anne attended his funeral.

I look at his picture from 1915 and remember the Ross family portrait from 47 years earlier—his jaunty stance at the end of the sofa, the sense I had of the closeness of the family. Who do we see in the thirteen year old of the childhood photograph? What is his relationship to the man turning sixty in the later photograph? It's the question I keep asking—without satisfactory answers—as I compare photographs taken across time.

The obituary offers me hints about his personality, though it is likely that only the positive aspects of anyone's personality make it into such a document and the accuracy and truth of the statements are not always reliable. Nonetheless, it claims that "from early manhood he was a most devoted member of the Presbyterian church, and for the last thirteen years had given conscientious service as an elder of the First Presbyterian church, where his interests, counsel, and untiring faith will be keenly missed." According to the obituary, among "his last works was the reorganization of the Presbyterian church choir, in whose behalf as its director were given those last atoms of his physical strength." I don't know to what extent the obit's final claim can be verified: "His life will be remembered as an example of irreproachable Christian fidelity." At the service a soloist sang "Lead Kindly Light" and "Abide with Me," identified as two of his favorite hymns.

Charles was the son of a Methodist minister and his wife's parents and grandparents had been active members of the Presbyterian Church in Cooperstown; Dr. Horace Lathrop, who died in 1905, ten years before this picture was taken, served as trustee of the church for a long time. Charles Ross seems always to have been a businessman—the 1880 census identifies him as a dry goods clerk in New York City and he seems to have been in business in Indianapolis before coming to Cooperstown; here he was at one time a partner in Smith & Ross, "meat dealers," and at his death in business with his son-in-law's father, Winfield Scott Root, in Root & Ross, "marble dealers" (tombstones). The nature of the business seems to have mattered little to him.

The thread of business that runs through that side of my family tree is of interest to me, as is the thread of Presbyterianism and, buried in the obituary, the thread of artistic endeavor. If these things are handed down—Charles's daughter Delia, my grandmother, would be known for her musical abilities, and her son, my father, would be both a businessman and a Presbyterian elder— then the threads, such as they are, are worthy of attention.

Based on what I see in this photograph of my great-grandfather Ross at sixty—the openness of his gaze, the calm of his posture, the trim of his apparel, the near-smile in his eyes and below his moustache-- how reliably can I claim for him contentment in his life, satisfaction with what he has and what he has accomplished, optimism about what the future holds for his family? Why do I feel I can? Am I, nudged by the claims of the obituary, reading his portrait with any degree of accuracy at all?

TESTIMONY

It's difficult not to characterize someone based on a solitary image of them in a family album. In the only photo I have of my grandparents' wedding the dour countenance of my great-grandfather Root glowers at the camera and it's hard for me not to encapsulate his personality based on that single picture. It makes me wish I could have the testimony of those who knew some of my ancestors, information that would broaden my understanding of them, and sometimes I can find it.

The biographical account of John Lothroppe in that family history quotes various figures about his life and character, and from time to time a quotation appears in other entries, likely taken from obituaries, as to the nature of certain individuals. The entry for Horace Lathrop, M. D., in the *Biographical Review* claims that he was then "one of the prominent men of the county in many respects, always taking an active interest in whatever tends to benefit the community and elevate his fellowmen"; attention is particularly paid to his involvement "in educational and religious matters." But the more compelling testimony comes in his obituary, from the *Freeman's Journal,* July 13, 1905, which opens: "The 'Beloved Physician' is no more!" The author, S.M.S., had known Dr. Lathrop for "a full half century" and claimed that "only the immediate family will miss him more than will his old friend." He quotes a patriotic acrostic poem written by the doctor and states: "He shirked no duty, private or public, imposed upon him. He was a man of decided opinions and views, which he did not hesitate to avow when called for, and at the same time was perhaps the most popular citizen of the village." He asserts, "He leaves a memory which is an inspiration and a most worthy example to others."

It takes a certain prominence to get such an obituary and it's hard to doubt the sincerity of the emotions and judgments expressed. This was my great-great grandfather, the father of my grandmother's mother. There's no way to know what effect he had on Mary Lathrop Ross or, through her, on my grandmother Betsy, but surely there was some.

More direct testimony on family members comes in a letter from Florence Root, my grandfather's sister, to my aunt Fran, my father's sister. Florence was two years older than Arthur. Of her mother, Evalina Pier Donaldson Root, Florence wrote:

> She attended a higher institution, in Ohio (I may remember the name sometime), which was ---------- Seminary, and paid her entrance fees by painting a large picture for them. I think she had done some teaching before as well as after she graduated from that institution. Part of the teaching was spent in a district where she "boarded around" a week at a time in one of the homes of the pupils whom she taught (going home for Sat. + Sundays). She told of going one place where the mother was weaving. The dishes from dinner had not been washed and she wondered how she could be there a whole 5 day period. But she finally left her weaving to get supper. Mother took her place and did some weaving while waiting for supper and when the family sat down to eat, she said everything was in spick + span order, the supper was excellent—so she had a happy week there.

Oral history, the anecdotal evidence of a life which may be no certain evidence at all, gives me merely a glimpse into a life long in the past. Evalina was born in 1860, Florence in 1893, and the letter recording the memory of what her mother told her once was written late in Florence's life (she died at 102, in 1995). The event in Evalina's teaching would have taken place sometime in the early 1880s and been told to Florence twenty or thirty years later: Evalina died in 1940. By the time Florence passed on the story to my aunt, some ninety to one hundred years had passed from the original event.

Still, Florence's testimony transmits a certain sense of Evalina's character. It also provides a detail I had not known: "Mother, as you have heard many times I think, was a real artist— our house in Nelson Ave had a lot of her pictures on our walls." I'd like to have seen those pictures, which apparently were passed on to her son Charles.

Of her father, W. S. Root, Florence believes that, as a boy, he attended Gilbertsville Academy. Gilbertsville, to the west of Cooperstown, was the center of activity among the Roots for generations. One area dominated by Root family farms was known as Rootsville, and all of Scott and Evalina's children were born in the Town of Butternuts. Florence writes:

> I think I had just passed my 7th birthday (Dec 1893) in the spring 1901, when we moved into Gilbertsville from the farm. We lived 1st in a house up above the Academy for several years until Father bought a house down the street that leads to the Frone farm, and lived there until Father was elected County Clerk of Otsego Co. when we moved to Cooperstown. I <u>think</u> I was 12 at that time—anyway Charles graduated from High School in 1907, Donald in 1908, I in 1909, but I took 1 yr. postgraduate before entering Smith College 1910. Father was County Clerk for 2 terms (don't remember the # of years).

W. Scott Root's obituaries, in both the *Freeman's Journal* and the *Oneonta Star* for May 31, 1950, record that he "operated a coal and feed business at Wellsbridge from 1892 to 1901," then served as postmaster at Gilbertsville from 1901 to 1905, and was elected Otsego County Clerk in 1905, serving until 1911. The county clerk position brought him and his family to the house on Nelson Avenue where his teen-aged children completed their growing up. The Nelson Avenue house was a few blocks away from the Chestnut Street home of the Ross family, where my grandmother was growing up.

> Florence continues her reminiscence of her father with an anecdote that took place when she graduated from Smith College.

> He bought his first auto (Paige) before I graduated in 1914. He + Mother brought Arthur with them up to the Graduation exercise. On the way home we brought a college friend (Dorothy Thorne) with us. They first talked of spending the night somewhere on the way, but as we got down almost to "home" country he decided we could make it, so we went on. However, we came to a parting of the roads—on the right it went up a rather steep hill, on the left it went on the level. He had slowed down almost to a stop, trying to decide, + when he changed gears into low, he made a mistake + went into reverse! (I can't remember whether it was dark by that time—perhaps nearly dark). Back we went—all 5 of us perfectly silent—but soon the back of the car was rising as we crossed the road backing up a bank, till the front wheels

21

got to the ditch + stopped! Mother said afterwards, the last time she had looked over on the left side the bank went <u>down</u> + she had visions of all of us being thrown out, but we were all intact. Arthur + Father got out and pulled the car out + we all got in, took the low road, and got home safely! No damage done to car or us.

It's a small story and not particularly eventful, but interesting because it has stuck in Florence's memory. Through it we learn that her young brother was called "Arthur," not Art or Artie; in 1914 he turned 19.

Florence shares one other memory of her childhood with Aunt Fran:

> While W.S.R. was county clerk, he bought a nice motor boat that was big enough for us all to ride, and during the summer we would frequently take our supper out and eat it in the boat out on the lake. Mother fixed a shredded wheat box for each of the 6 of us, with the dessert on the bottom, + 1st course on the top so we ate in that order, so we did not have to take things out except as we ate. Those boxes were the kind that had (I think) 12 "cakes" of the shredded wheat in a box. We had it almost every morning for breakfast because we liked it! Mother saved the boxes for our picnics.

Cooperstown is situated at the foot of nine-mile long Lake Otsego, the source of the Susquehanna River. It is a beautiful lake and I try to imagine that boat filled with the Root family rocking gently in mid-lake as the family members eat their dinner from shredded wheat boxes, layer by layer.

What stays in our memories, readily available for recall, is not always the most significant or profound events, those best able to define us in an image, but they surface details that capture moments in our lives that the historical records can never reveal. I place these stories beside an image of my great-grandfather scowling in my grandparents' wedding photo, and wonder how they modify the impression I have of him.

The stories also revive in me the realization of the way letters, diaries, and journals silently offer a chance for a reader to "hear" the voices of their writers, an alternative to examining images as a way to get to know someone. My Great-Aunt Florence, for years a Presbyterian missionary in Korea, was someone I only met in person a few very brief times in my youth and I don't remember those meetings well. Luckily, a book about her missionary work, *Great Is Thy Faithfulness: The Life and Times of Florence Elizabeth Root,* by Ronald P. Detrick, has a few images to refresh my memory. The book says little about her childhood and family connections; it's the letters to my aunt that bring her to life for me and make me feel I know her, at least a little. Through her testimony I begin to sense a connection to the family that my grandfather came from.

FAMILY BUDNACK

Stanislaw Burdnzak was a family pioneer as fully as John Lothroppe or John Roote was. Like those men uprooting themselves from the land of their ancestors and ties to the family that gave them birth, he immigrated to America seeking the chance to build a new life and the opportunity to escape the old one. I know this not on the strength of anyone's testimony but rather from the bare bones of the circumstances.

What I know of the circumstances is scant but to my mind compelling: Stanislaw and Jaidwega Burdnzak and their three children, Mary, Frances, and Joseph (it's likely the children's birthnames were somewhat different in the old country), left Germany in 1892 and settled in western New York state. At the time of his departure, and for a hundred years before that, Poland had been divided between Prussia, Austria-Hungary, and Russia, its existence scoured from maps and its inhabitants subject to discrimination of varying harshness by its three imperial overlords. The western third of Poland, then considered part of Prussia, before Prussia united other German states to form Germany, was considered a space for expansion of the German people; as Americans and other colonizers had done with the land of North America once occupied by native tribes, the local inhabitants were displaced by growing numbers of outsiders encouraged to find homes in the new extension of national territory. The occupiers treated the occupied as conquerors usually treat the conquered: the language of the occupied was assumed inferior and obsolete and the language of the occupier was required for schooling and communication; names of cities and towns and rivers were changed; conscription into national service drew heavily on those who otherwise were not regarded as full-fledged citizens.

The history of Poland is a sad history in this regard. It endured decades of domination and occupation by neighboring powers: the long, shameful tripartite division of the country during the eighteenth and nineteenth centuries, lasting until the collapse of Germany and the Austro-Hungarian empire at the end of World War I; the sudden occupation and annexation by resurgent Nazi Germany after only twenty years of freedom; forty years of Soviet domination after World War II. It is a sign of Polish tenacity that the Poles still think of themselves as a national people and, finally free at last, have artfully reconstructed their obliterated landscape.

But in 1892, when Stanley Budnack was a subject of the King of Prussia, he and his wife somehow gathered up their three children, ages five, three, and two, and departed for a new and better world. At the time of emigration Stanley was 31, Hedwig 26. Between 1894 and 1909 she gave birth to eight more children, all American born, her child-bearing having lasted twenty-four years. My grandmother, Anna, born in January 1900, was their third daughter and their seventh child.

I know nothing of their journey or the means by which they were able to afford it and arrange it and find their way to Niagara County, in western New York. The Polish-American community in the Buffalo and Niagara Falls area is large and active, and no doubt connections to people there drew them to this particular place of settlement. Hedwig died in 1919, after the end of the First World War liberated Poland; Stanley died in 1945, when Poland was liberated from Germany once more.

I was three when Stanley died, and I have no memory of him. That's why the photos matter, because they connect me back to the vanished. This picture, a candid snapshot of Stanley on a farm, likely their farm in Niagara County, looking like the burly peasant immigrant he was, is one I value almost as much as the single family portrait I have of the Budnacks. It seems to capture something of the spirit of the man, perhaps only a glimpse and only a single facet. But looking at him in his work clothes raising his hat jauntily in the air and smiling at the camera, I think of him as a man who had the resolve and the strength to bring his family to a foreign country and start over from nearly scratch.

It's not inconsequential to me that, without that spirit, that strength and resolve, I would not be here. He was my great-grandfather and his decisions and actions set in motion the sequence of events that led to my grandmother and my mother being in the world in the place that they were when I came into the world.

*   *   *

I guess at the date of this photograph, possibly 1910. The whole of the Budnack family is here, and then some. I have census records from 1900 and 1910 and can determine some of the identities from estimating ages and recognizing some, though by no means all, of the faces.

The couple seated at the center of the photograph, as befits their status as matriarch and patriarch, are my great-grandparents, the parents of my mother's mother. The man is Stanley Budnack, to give him the final name he lived under, after all the efforts by clerks and government officials to Americanize his Polish names. The boy on his lap, I assume, is his youngest son, William, a year old. The woman is Jaidwega, later Hedwick, later Hedwig Budnack, whose maiden name I'm still trying to uncover and verify. In the row behind them, the second figure from the left, the smiling young woman, is their oldest child, Mary, about 25; their second child, another daughter, Frances, about 23, is the curly-haired figure

26

standing behind Stanley and William. My grandmother, then about 10, is standing to Mary's left. I can see in this photograph her resemblance to her mother, something I never knew before. In the front row are two more of her sisters, Florence and Josephine; my guess is that they are the two in stockings, Florence on the left, Josie the blonde, youngest daughter on the right.

The Budnacks had eleven children, five girls and six boys. I think I recognize Ambrose, then around 8, in the short blonde boy in knickers on the far right. As for Joseph, then 20, Michael, 16, John, 14, and Stanley Jr., then 12, I see family resemblances among three of the standing young men, maybe Joe behind Ambrose, Michael behind Anna, Stanley Jr. to Mary's right, John in the chair in his parents' row. Two of the remaining four young men may be beaus or spouses of Mary and Frances; the woman holding the baby may be Joe's wife. I have no idea who the two other children or the older woman or the two other young men may be.

This is another of those photographs that have come to me late in life, one I value for giving me a view of a large cast of characters from the now distant past. Any of those people I ever knew, a few of whom I remember fairly well, were in their forties and fifties when I met them. My grandmother, here a solemn little girl, was 42 when I was born, her sister Mary 58, her sister Frances 56, her brother Ambrose, who everyone called "Ham," 40. Only the younger sisters, Florence and Josie, were in their late thirties. It pleases me to be able to pick out among these faces those people I knew only in their maturity. In the '50s and '60s these were the people whose funerals we were constantly attending, the ones whose spouses and children we of my generation seldom recognized.

The picture is a historical artifact, the kind you might see on the wall of the Niagara County Historical Museum, the kind we study for the quaintness of the clothing (look at that bow tie, look at the collars on the women's blouses, the floppy bows in the little girls' hair) or for the expressions on the subjects' faces (why does the man in the bowtie seem alarmed? Why is the blond boy so rigid? Why is the guy in the center looking so intently?). We study hairstyles and moustaches and clothing in such photos and think ourselves disconnected to those bygone eras. We use the term "bygone era" as if it was a common phrase for us.

If over a hundred years have passed since this picture was taken, it surely is historical. And yet I knew these people, I recognize something about the attitudes that Anna, Mary, Frances, Ambrose, and Josie display in the way they hold their heads, their bodies, their expressions on their faces. Though they are two and three generations removed from my generation, I recognize in some of their faces the generation that would intervene between theirs and mine. Something about Ham and the brother behind him reappears in my uncles Gene and Bobby; something about Mary and Frances is passed through my grandmother to my uncle Paul. There are mysterious threads of connection here, maybe only superficial links of appearance but maybe also hints of some other kind of linkage that can't be deciphered or recorded, only intuited or, more vaguely, felt.

The face that I read most closely, of course, the one that I use the "zoom in" feature on my laptop to enlarge again and again until the pixels blur, is Anna's face, my grandmother's face. And it occurs to me just as I write this, having tried to find my grandmother in Anna's features and expression, that Anna here is not my grandmother but a little girl with a big bow behind, rather than on top of, her head. She is someone who has no inkling of her future, the one I will know all the way to her death at 88, the one with her husband, her children, her grandchildren, her great-grandchildren.

The one with me in it.

I am connected to this historical photograph because I am part of the way the history that succeeded the photograph played itself out. This is a photograph of people who are now all dead, all departed, but it is also a photograph of the potential in people waiting to fulfill itself.

FAMILY LINDERMAN

My mother has handily labeled the people in the picture for the benefit of her own children. That must be the reason her own parents in the photo are identified as Gram and Grandpa, her own grandparents as G. Gram and G. Grandpa. My grandparents are easy for me to pick out and, even without the labels, I would have spotted them, on the left-hand end of the back row. But I wouldn't have been able to identify anyone else in the picture. I surmise, in part through resemblances, that the great-grandparents are my grandfather's parents, George and Mary Linderman. George is standing in the center of the back row and Grandpa's brother Al stands to his left; Grandpa's oldest sister, Lillian, George and Mary's first born, sits in front of Grandpa, and I'm fairly certain her husband Bill stands to my grandmother's left and her son is the little boy at bottom center. My grandfather's youngest brother, Ed, stands second to the end, but I can't determine the relationship of the other three people to the family, in spite of their names being clear on the picture. This photo must have been taken in front of my greatgrandparents' farmhouse; there's just enough of the front porch showing for me to identify it.

My grandparents look young in the picture, and I can only estimate the year it was taken—at the moment I don't know when they were married, but both were listed as living with their parents in the 1920 census and in 1921 their son Paul, my oldest uncle, was born. Since my grandmother doesn't look pregnant, I'd date it somewhere around 1919-1921, by the time she either was—or was regarded as—a member of the Linderman family. The shirtsleeves suggest it was a late spring or summer day, probably on a Sunday morning, around noon (white shirts on the men, their sleeves rolled up, the east-facing porch in shadow). Is there anything else I know about this photograph, anything else I can assume or deduce?

My great-grandfather, George Linderman (spelled Lindeman or Lindemann on some records) was born in Germany, purportedly near Hamburg, on May 25, 1867, and arrived at the Port of New York on November 3, 1884. I don't know how he found his way across the state to Western New York, but around 1891 he married a woman named Mary Meinke (or Miencke or Meinecke), who was herself born in New York, the daughter of parents born in Germany. My best guess is that she was the daughter of Charles and Mary Mienke, who emigrated in 1870, and was called Minnie in her childhood, as women named Mary often seem to have been. This all suggests that George and Mary met in the midst of a German emigrant population around Buffalo. Their first child, Lillie, was born in 1892, their second Alfred (or Alfie) in 1895, and their third, Arthur, my mother's father, in 1897, in North Tonawanda, a suburb of Buffalo right on the line between Erie and Niagara counties. A fourth child, Edward, was born in 1906, likely as a surprise.

At the time of this photograph, then, my grandfather would have been around 23 and my grandmother 20. Both came from emigrant stock, from families choosing to leave Prussia or Germany, whichever it was called when they left; both came from farm families on the Niagara Frontier; both were American born though no doubt European relatives were in the armies Americans had been fighting in Europe in the years before their marriage.

As it happens three of my four maternal great-grandparents were still alive when I was born, though with my great-grandfathers the period we overlapped on this earth was short. Stanley Budnack died in 1945; George Linderman died in 1946; Mary Linderman lived on until 1963, though my memories of her are few and vague.

It strikes me their deaths, those of Stanley and Jaidwega and George, closed the last of our family's links to the old world. Did it make a difference that my mother's parents were first-generation Americans and my father's parents were many generations removed from their European origins? Did it make a difference that my mother's parents were the children of farm laborers and housewives and my father's parents the descendants of a long line of ministers and teachers and businessmen? If who we are and where we come from affects the way we see ourselves and our world, then these origins matter, and when people with such varied origins and traditions come together, it must affect the way they see each other and the life they intend to make together.

*   *   *

I guess the date of the photograph to be sometime in 1929. My mother's labeling of the people in the picture helps. On the left side of the canoe are my uncle Gene, the youngest of my mother's brothers, four years younger, and my grandmother Anna. Gene looks to be between one and two years old, which would make my grandmother twenty-nine. The woman in the middle of the boat is my grandmother's second oldest sister, Frances, thirteen years older than my grandmother; Frances' son William is beside her. On the right side, at the bow of the canoe, the two somber children are my mother, Marie, then around six, and her oldest brother, Paul, then around eight. Bobby, the brother who was born between Marie and Gene, is not in the picture.

My grandmother was forty-two when I was born. I have almost no memory of her except in a loose patterned dress and never knew her when she was young. The dress she wears in this photograph is unusually smart to be part of my grandmother's wardrobe and she herself seems slim and attractive, a pretty young mother. Except for the labels across the top of the picture I would not have recognized my mother, with her blonde hair and serious

31

expression and bright frock, or my uncle Gene, though with study I would have identified my uncle Paul and my great-aunt Frances and my grandmother.

From the words on the side of the bow, I determine that this was taken at Olcott, the resort town on Lake Ontario, four miles north of Newfane, a dozen miles north of Lockport. Olcott Beach was once a popular place for summer picnics, swimming, fishing, and boating; its long pier, shaped like a backwards L, protected the beach area from the rougher Ontario waves and gave fishermen a distant semi-isolated perch away from their families. At one time two amusement parks offered a host of rides and games—Ferris wheels, carousels, a line-up of prize-offering games of chance, and a penny arcade with pinball games and silent nickelodeon movies. Apparently the area also had a tourist photo studio, where families posed in this canoe set against a backdrop of a river or lake scene, an oar positioned in painted water in the foreground, and a photographer on hand to cajole everyone into the appearance of good cheer.

This is a scene I can partly identify with, because in the summers of my childhood we went often to Olcott and for many years Harrison Radiator, where my grandfather and eventually my uncles all worked, held an annual employees' picnic at Krull Park, overlooking the lake. I can assume that this was a Sunday outing of the two sisters and their families, and I can be almost certain that my grandfather is down on the pier fishing, as I remember him doing most Sundays when I was among those going to Olcott. There may be more to the event than a typical Sunday, since William and Paul are sporting ties and my grandmother and great-aunt seem somewhat stylishly dressed for a day at Olcott, even if they all had been to church.

Even more than the family portraits of my young grandparents with their families, the figures so unknown as to be historical, this picture changes the way I see the image. I know who these people are, not through a process of deduction, but through personal experience. All were older then, but they were in the world I was in when I was in it, every one of them. I can match up their older, adult faces with the younger faces I see here. Except for William, I remember when each of them left the world I was in.

Somehow, seeing them here as they once appeared in a world in which I had no existence or, for that matter, into which none of them could ever imagine my coming, I feel less disembodied than with those earlier family portraits, of all those people I never met or, despite having met them, have no concrete memory of being on the same earth with them. It's as if I am in the distant mist of that backdrop, far off, invisible, not merely so much more likely but almost—though I know that it was never the case—almost inevitable.

MEMORY

Here's the problem with memory.

In my childhood, I am taken to visit people in the country. At the time I was of a certain age and a certain state of knowledge. Perhaps someone explained who the people we were visiting were; perhaps they assumed I knew what they knew. I may be going along because of some special family occasion, but it may also have been simply a routine visit. It was some time in the mid-1940s. I'm in the company of my grandparents, people who grew up in rural western New York, lived on small farms in the country for the first twenty years or so of their lives, and now live in a small industrialized city less than a dozen miles away. We're visiting older people, whom my grandparents come back to visit, people who emigrated from "the Old Country" shortly before the turn of the twentieth century and whose children, including my grandparents, are the first American-born members of their family line.

But I was talking about memory. On this visit I'm trying to remember I am a child of, what? three? four? years of age stopping at a house in the country where older relatives of some kind live. As an adult, I've been on those back roads since then, though only intermittently and with other purposes in mind, and I don't know what overlays of images interfere with my memory of the house and the land. I vaguely visualize a two-story white house, with bushes grown up around it, and a low porch a step above the ground leading to the front door. I remember a central room with a table in the middle, a lace doily on the table and perhaps a flowerpot or a squat kerosene lamp with a clear chimney. Memory doesn't help much; I think I see a black cast iron woodstove against the wall in that room, but in the same space I also see stairs leading to the upper level. Doors to other rooms lead off the central room and the kitchen, with another woodstove, larger and broader, against the outside wall. The center of the house seems to be the only space I know, though somehow that staircase looks narrow and steep and I feel that I've been up it, walked around second floor bedrooms of which I have no memory. There's a back door to that central room, and light comes in from the back yard through a screen door that leads to another small low porch. Is there a rusty hand pump for a well on or near that porch? Am I bringing in memories from other old farmhouses into the fabric of my memory of this house?

So how can I reconstruct the memory of this visit? How many visits did I make and how often did I make them? What of repetition, of routine, shapes this memory, which seems like one memory but possibly was many memories? At first I imagine driving up in a large rounded automobile, like the green and white 1951 or 1952 Chevy my grandfather owned that eventually became my first car, but if the memory comes from the 1940s it must have been a different car, perhaps the big black one I've seen only in photographs in which I stand on the running board or sit on the fender. (They are black and white photos and, in memory, I only visualize the car in black and white.)

I seem to recall parking on the lawn along the road; perhaps there were other cars in the driveway. It likely is a Sunday, when the men would not be working, and surely my grandfather drove, my grandmother next to him, my mother in the back seat with me. My father would not be there—he was still in the Marines; I barely knew I had a father. I guess my grandmother's younger sister Josie and her husband Leo have driven down as well, and perhaps others of her siblings, almost none of whom I know by name. I have a sense of bustle in the house, but a sense of confinement as well. Was there a barn? Was there only a small yard? I have no memory of ever having roamed the property. Did I hear words spoken in a foreign language, German perhaps, or was the accent the older people spoke with as good as a foreign language to me?

This is the problem with memory. This visit happened but I can recollect none of it clearly. I think an old man, taciturn and uncommunicative, sat sternly apart on the porch for part of the time. I can almost see him, sort of, but wouldn't recognize him if he stepped before me now unchanged from that day. But perhaps I was shy and withdrawn before strangers and perhaps because I was not the first of his great-grandchildren, as I was the first grandchild for both sets of grandparents, he was less interested in me. I feel as if my great-grandfather and my grandfather sat together on the porch and said little, simply appreciated sitting quietly on a Sunday as men did in those days after a week of work. I might have been only interested in finding other children to play with, but except possibly for some older girls, like Aunt Frances's daughters or Aunt

Florence's daughter Carol, there may have been no others in my generation then, or at least none there in the country at that moment. I may have been bored and intimidated by the strangeness of the people and the place and tried not to draw attention to myself. Or maybe not.

Is this all that's left of this memory? Vague images of carpets and tables and walls, of people's shapes and coloring rather than faces and names and dialogue and actions? Who knew I would want this memory? Who knew that so many decades after this visit I would want to draw on it for some sense of who I was then and where I came from and how these old people influenced and affected the generations that followed them? Is this memory clearly stored somewhere in the recesses of my brain, like some fresh digital image I could see in all its detail and clarity if only I possessed the software to download it? Or is it a corrupt file, a dingy, dust covered, mouse-nibbled fragment bleeding into other memories, past all hope of recovery and interpretation? Is this what memory ends up being—this pile of useless and incomprehensible fragments? Is this what I'm working so hard to continue piling up?

When I first wrestled with this memory, I believed somehow that the old people we were visiting were my grandmother's parents. Then I began tracking down some facts. My great-grandmother Hedwig died at age 53 in 1919, around the time my grandmother and grandfather married but before my own mother was born. Hedwig was never part of my mother's memories or mine. My great-grandfather Stanley died in 1945, when he was 84 and I was around three. My grandfather's parents lived longer. Great-grandfather George died in 1946, when I was nearly four and he was around 80; my great-grandmother Mary was then 74 and lived to be 90, dying in 1963. I was 20 or 21 when she died and still I have no memory of her, only an image from a photograph of my mother standing next to me in a gravel parking lot by a small country church that must have been taken at my great-grandmother's memorial service. These facts make me want to say that the house in my memory was the Lindermans' house on RFD #8 in the Town of Newfane, but I wonder how much my factual knowledge is skewing my understanding of my memory. If indeed my great-grandfather—either of them—is in the memory, then it is a very early memory, perhaps the earliest I can retrieve, however patchy it may be.

36

What is the purpose and point of memory? It no doubt developed as an evolutionary skill that helped determine survival—those who remembered when fruit would be ripe or where the carcass for scavenging was stored or which kind of mushroom killed and which didn't tended to live longer—and led to agriculture and civilization, the by-products of memory-dependent knacks for repetition and planning; our memories kept developing until we had an expansive, indiscriminate, and involuntary tendency to remember. Consider what we remember without effort: the lyrics to "Itsy Bitsy Teenie Weenie Yellow Polka-Dot Bikini" and "Mairzy Doats"; the words to radio commercials for Brylcreem and Wildroot Crème Oil and Philip Morris cigarettes and scores of television ads; the time you signed someone else's name in a yearbook instead of your own and how the entire class laughed about it; batting averages or box scores or win-loss records or statistics from sports you neither played nor attended nor watched; the prices of products you have no intention of buying; the kinds of candy in the vending machines in the Rialto theater in 1949; the relationship between the Lone Ranger and the Green Hornet and the meaning of words like "Bundolo" and "Kreegah", "Bolgani" and "Tarmangani" and "Mangani" in ape language and the identities of Shere Khan and Ka and Balu and Bagheera, of Simba and Tantor, and the titles of the first eight Bomba books in order; the names of all fifty states (a college friend could recite the names of senior and junior senators from all fifty states); the birth names of Rock Hudson and John Wayne and Judy Garland and countless others. If memory, once crucial for preserving and developing our species, now approximates the function of an automatic vacuum cleaner of unselected information, sucking up the inanities of bumper stickers and the poetry of bathroom walls as well as the identities of poisonous insects and reptiles and the procedures for changing a tire, then it is merely an accident of evolution that we also remember love and pain, joy and loss, the distinguishing personalities and moments and features of our lives—all the things that make us think we are individuals with unique identities, that make us self-conscious about our own existence, our own consciousness of being. It may well be that memory is, in the end, irrelevant, just an evolutionary parlor-trick. If so, what are we do with all the snippets and patches of memory that flash across our synapses unbidden, offering no resolution to their meaning? What are we do with all the fragments that refuse us further access, like random jigsaw pieces for which we have insufficient evidence to complete the puzzle's picture?

LINEAGE

So, as I mentioned before, in regard to lineage, there are two questions to answer: Who were the people you came from? How did who they were influence the kind of people your parents became?

Knowing the names and the pertinent dates and addresses of your ancestors doesn't really say much about who they were. Looking at etchings or portraits or photographs allows you to make assumptions about their personalities—attempt to read their character—but, as any study of photographs of yourself reveals, an instantaneous image taken at a particular moment says little about the complex character of the individual in the image. While others in the photo laugh and smile and seem to behave in concert with one another, your eyes are closed, your face expressionless; has the camera captured your disaffection from the group, your isolation or lack of involvement, or has it merely caught you in a moment of acid reflux, a reaction to the sun's glare, a sudden realization of spinach on your teeth, preoccupation with your companions' arrangement in the camera frame, ignorance of the joke all the others heard? If you can't reliably read the image of yourself in a moment you recently lived through, how you can accurately read the image of another taken in your absence, perhaps before you were born?

The only image I have of my great-grandfather W. S. Root is that scowling figure standing apart from the smiling group gathered for my grandparents' wedding. Was he contentious all day long, as family legend would have it, and should I think him a gruff, dissatisfied figure throughout his life? What I need are the testimonies of witnesses, but the witnesses to his life are all but entirely unavailable now. I pursue whatever fragments of documentary evidence I might find, but even that can be suspect. No obituary I've ever seen has stated of anyone, "He was consistently a pain in the ass to everyone who knew him, and of his loss his children only wish it would have come sooner." No, obituaries are routinely positive spins on the deceased's life, akin to a defense attorney's closing argument hoping at least for leniency if not acquittal. You can hope that it's largely accurate but in a couple hundred words it will mostly be about names and dates and jobs and hobbies, offering little insight into personality or character.

So, what can the annals of lineage and a few random photographs and scarcer documents tell me about those who came before my grandparents? In *Nothing to Be Frightened Of,* Julian Barnes, analyzing the comfort having children is supposed to bring to those who fear their own eventual deaths (he doubts it), notes that the "main argument . . . is that your children 'carry you on' after your death: you will not be entirely extinguished, and foreknowledge of this brings consolation at a conscious or subconscious level." (He also doubts that he and his brother are "carrying on" their parents.) Assuming "that the proposed intergenerational portage occurs in a manner satisfactory to all," he wonders,

> How far does such "carrying on" go? One generation, two, three? What happens when you reach the first generation born after you are dead, the one with no possible memory of you, and for whom you are mere folklore? Will you be carried on by them, and will they know that this is what they are doing?

Despite Barnes' cynicism about his own upbringing, it seems to me he asks a vital question, the one buried at the heart of any nature versus nurture argument.

Am I carrying on any part of the great-grandparents I never met or met only in infancy and how will I know that's what I'm doing? It's the question at the heart of lineage. It's the question I'm searching the annals of my ancestors to answer.

To know what I might be carrying on, I review my notes to learn the careers of my ancestors, their work choices, their level of education. Much of this information is hard to pin down, absent a collection of school and college degrees carefully maintained. Some figures on my father's side of the family, like Rev. John Lothroppe, educated at Queen's College, Cambridge, or Dr. Horace Lathrop, educated at Hartwick Seminary and Hamilton College, or Professor John Chester Donaldson, educated at Hamilton College, clearly have educated backgrounds, as do some with specific degrees, like Joseph Lothropp, who left an extensive library in his will, and Rev. Benjamin Lathrop, apparently a self-taught Baptist minister as well as a blacksmith, and Rev. William Ross, perhaps educated in Ireland before emigration. A number of the women such men married were the daughters of clergymen and doctors, and some, like Delia Ann Paddock, Dr. Horace Lathrop's wife, had written a significant funeral oration and Evalina Pier Donaldson, daughter of a professor, granddaughter of a lawyer and judge, graduated from Granville Female College in Ohio and taught for a while before marrying W. Scott Root. My grandparents, Arthur Root and Betsy Ross, attended college, he at Hamilton, she at Albany State Teacher's college, but neither received degrees, dropping out because of service during World War I. Betsy, it turns out, nonetheless was a short story writer and a columnist self-taught in psychology.

That lineage also has its share of individuals who achieved some prominence and some material success. The Root line is filled with farmers who were also businessmen. At one point an area of Otsego County called Rootville housed a collective of farms and a successful dairy and cheese-making operation. My great-grandfather started several different businesses in the area, and my grandfather's entire career was settled into management for the New York Telephone Company. In addition there is a strand of service to the church and the community, involvement in elective and appointed government positions, both local and national, and involvement in civic life.

I can't trace my mother's side of the family very far back. I only know that my great-grandfathers were farmers or farm laborers and that my great-grandmothers were housewives. What they or their forebears did in Prussia or Germany or Poland, I can't say. But I can identify a strand of responsibility, of willingness to work hard, provide for the well-being of one's family.

Do any of these things qualify as something you carry on? If I say of myself that I seem to be responsible, willing to work hard, tend to provide for my family's well-being, and that I'm college-educated and continually write, would any of my ancestors feel that I was carrying on their legacy? Looking at me and my life, is it apparent who my ancestors were?

On a biological level the sense that we carry on our ancestors is demonstrable—all we need to do is check our DNA and hope to back that up with notable similarities in appearance: the same kind of face, the same kind of body, the same corporeal flaws and idiosyncrasies. I recognize my sons-in-law in some of my grandchildren, my daughters in others. That's the kind of carrying on that we have no control over—the kinds of traits that surface even if you never know who your biological parents are. Julian Barnes acknowledges traits he recognizes as his father's: the angle at which he sits at a table, the hang of his jaw, his incipient baldness pattern, traits more or less built-in by the happenstance of who his male parent was. Yet, in a 2008 interview in *The Telegraph,* Barnes mentions traits that arise from intimate association with that parent, non-biological traits; he claims, "Temperamentally, I have a lot in common with my father. I don't like argument. [. . .] I would retreat into silence rather than argue and rage and storm. I think I have that from my father." In his book he admits also to sharing "a particular polite laugh that he emits when pretending to be amused." These are small features of personality but they are features Barnes is carrying on. They aren't simply a matter of happenstance; the biological and psychological elements he shares with his father are a matter of lineage, some of which—if not all—his father likely carried on from his grandfather.

Any of us hoping to acquire any level of certainty about the sources of such traits would need to look as closely as we can at whatever evidence of lineage we can find.

Interlude: 281 Cottage Street

My grandparents' house at 281 Cottage Street had a small, enclosed front porch; I barely remember anyone using it at all, though there were upholstered couches on it and some other furniture. The doorway in the center of the porch led to the living room, where I remember a burgundy corduroy davenport along the stairs, a couple of upholstered chairs in the other corners, each of them seemingly permanently designated for my grandfather and my grandmother. Near the porch door stood a large wooden console for the radio with a flat surface on top where they kept the crank-operated Victrola, with its heavy arm and needle for playing 78 rpm recordings, mostly my mother's collection of swing and big band music. The radio was the centerpiece of entertainment, however. After supper, my grandmother would scurry in from the kitchen to make sure the radio was tuned to the right station to hear the opening strains of the William Tell Overture and the stirring start to *The Lone Ranger*. We listened as well to *Sergeant Preston of the Yukon, The Green Hornet, Mr. Keen, Tracer of Lost Persons, The Shadow, The Fat Man, Fibber McGee and Molly, Duffy's Tavern, The Great Gildersleeve, Jack Armstrong the All-American Boy, Gangbusters, The FBI in Peace and War, Edgar Bergen and Charlie McCarthy, Rogue's Gallery, Richard Diamond, Private Detective, John Steele, Adventurer,* and dozens more, though I suspect that many of these programs I remember only from opening lines as I was carried up to bed or from snatches of music and dialogue that wafted up the stairs as I dozed off.

The stairs were on the north wall of the living room and I remember how much my grandparents hated our climbing on the bannister and jumping onto the couch below, something we only got away with when the adults were in the kitchen, past the dining room and toward the back of the house. The kitchen was a long narrow room, with a wall of floor-to-ceiling closets on one end, near the cellar stairs and the side entrance to the house, and a floor-to-ceiling bank of cabinets at the far end, past the gauntlet of stove, sink, refrigerator, and steel table and chairs. The dining room, next to the kitchen, had the good wooden table, covered with a tablecloth, and matching wooden chairs, a china cabinet and extra tables for setting up dishes during large family meals. The rear of the dining room led to a downstairs bedroom, where visiting children often napped or visitors' coats were laid on the bed; I'm not certain but I think that it was my grandparents' bedroom. I seem to recall having to be quiet because Grampa was sleeping in there, perhaps because he had worked a night shift or overtime at Harrison Radiator, and I don't remember them going up the stairs to go to bed.

Much of what I remember of the downstairs, I suspect, has been reinforced by visits over the years beyond the times I lived in that house. The upstairs is less clear in my memory, though I can see the landing two steps up from the living room floor, the turn and the steep ascent—these were the stairs I would have climbed as a toddler and have learned to negotiate in early childhood—and the hallway at the top. The bathroom was the first door to the left, the bathtub on the left as you entered, the sink on the right, the toilet beyond the sink below a small window on the back wall, and a clothes hamper— always layered with a mix of magazines—and maybe some shelving opposite the toilet.

As I remember it, there were two bedrooms upstairs. I can't seem to recall which room I slept in, perhaps because, at one time or another, I may have slept in both of them. My instinct is to say that I slept in the smaller, back bedroom, perhaps shared it with my mother, but where did my uncle Gene sleep or his two older brothers if they still lived at home? I have an image of several beds in that large front bedroom and suspect that, as the children grew up over the years that the family was in that house—they moved out of the dinky house in Lowertown and into this larger house with the huge back yard in the south end of Lockport when my mother was still a toddler—the boys had the big bedroom, my mother had the small bedroom, and my grandparents took the bedroom downstairs. I also seem to remember a blanket dividing off part of that large bedroom, like the walls of Jericho in *It Happened One Night*, but I can't be sure of the memory. Whatever the arrangement, it may have shifted many times, as the boys moved out, as my mother married and her husband moved in, as she had first me and then my sister and finally my brother, all while she lived in that house with my grandparents.

One part of the upstairs sticks in my mind. In the northwest corner of that front bedroom was a small closet, set in the space between the west wall (the wall facing Cottage Street) and the point where the ceiling above the stairs slanted up behind the north wall. I think there were drawers built into the low space to the right of the closet entrance—I'm not certain it actually had a door—but the unique feature of the closet was the way it angled up above the stairs until it met the floor of the attic. The entrance to the attic was in the hallway, and hardly ever used, though some items were stored in it over the years. The wedge of space above the stairs was too sharply slanted to hold very much securely, but blankets and boxes were stored there and it was possible to clamber over them and slip back into the darkness of the wedge, especially if you were a very little boy. It was eventually a forbidden area—my grandmother dreaded the notion of a child falling through the ceiling and tumbling down the stairs—but my mother and my uncles would have known about it and at some point someone (probably Uncle Gene) introduced me to it and I would find myself longing to climb up into it and move around a narrowly circumscribed, almost womblike space. In later years my mother told me that, once, she and my grandmother got preoccupied with something and lost track of me, then suddenly realized they didn't know where I was. A frantic search of the house didn't turn me up and they were about to scour the neighborhood even though they could imagine no way I could have left the house, when someone thought to check the closet, where I turned out to be sleeping in the wedge.

Both entrances to the house were on its north wall, facing the driveway. The one closest to the street was the one above a short set of steps leading to that enclosed front porch. The other was set at midpoint in the north wall and opened directly onto the driveway. This was the entrance we most often used, because it led to a landing midway between the basement and the kitchen, where we could hang coats and mittens and hats and deposit wet or muddy boots and shoes. Just to the side of the door was a milk slot, a small square space in the wall with an interior and an exterior door that allowed the milkman to open the outside door and replace empty milk bottles with full ones and allowed us to open the inner door to pick them up or return them. I know too that ice was delivered door-to-door in my time, although I don't recall if it was delivered to us or if we had replaced our icebox (as everyone continued to call it) with a refrigerator that created its own frigid temperatures (I believe we owned a Frigidaire, which was always pronounced Friguh-dare—the realization that the brand name was invented from the descriptive "frigid air" was an early indicator that I would be interested in the uses of language in later years).

The first story of the two-story house was thus raised above the ground and the basement windows were high in the walls, just at the level of the ground outside. One window served as an opening for another historical detail: coal delivery. From time to time a coal truck would pull into our driveway—this happened across the street at what became our family home as well, in the early years that we lived there—and a man would pull out a chute, attach it to the rear of the truck, then open the cellar window and push the low end of the chute inside. We would hear the hydraulic whine as the bed of the truck lifted and the gate on the truck end of the chute opened and the force of gravity sent chunks of coal down the chute. I liked to watch the coal rumbling through the chute and then run into the basement to see it tumble into the coalbin, the dark section of the basement set off with high wooden walls to contain the coal and the coal dust and to provide easy shoveling to the maw of the furnace a few steps away from the entrance to the coalbin. I had been warned not to step into the coalbin for fear of being buried in coal, but I always watched for a chunk of coal to tumble out of the bin onto the basement floor so that I could pick it up, hold this glittering black lump in my hand. I sometimes went into the basement with my grandfather or my uncle when they stoked the furnace and fed coal into it, or cleaned out the ashes. Among my concerns about growing up over the years was a dread of having to keep the coal furnace burning and carrying out the impossibly heavy ashcans for the dustmen to pick up.

My grandparents' basement was clean and dry. My grandmother was a stickler for cleanliness and made certain none of the house was cluttered, including the basement. Toward the rear of the basement she kept the food she canned herself over the summer for meals throughout the winter; the shelves were neatly lined in a dark, cool, and somewhat ominous windowless space. At the rear of the basement was my grandfather's workroom. Another intimidation about growing up and taking on the responsibilities of manhood: all the tools men had to know how to use. My grandfather was an adept carpenter, a handyman who took care of most household repairs, and his tools were clean and neatly arranged in his workroom. What I particularly remember were his molds for sinkers—he was also an avid fisherman—and how my uncle Gene and my grandfather would sometimes melt lead and fill a mold and later produce minnow-shaped weights to attach to their fishing lines to pull their hooks underwater. There may have been—I believe there was—a collection of different sized hooks and a variety of fishing lures down there as well.

But my grandmother's preserves and my grandfather's tools, partly because they were housed so far back in the darker recesses of the basement and partly because they were so adamant about no one playing around them, rarely received any attention from me. I was, however, obsessed with the barber's chair in the center of the large, well-lit area in the front of the basement. My grandfather had been, at one time, a barber—my grandmother's accusation against my father's parents, that they objected to their son marrying a barber's daughter, was grounded in that fact—but for all of my childhood was employed, like his three sons after him, like my brother after them, at Harrison Radiator, the division of General Motors that dominated the economy of the city and whose main plant occupied several blocks of property in the downtown. For years, however, my grandfather continued to barber for family and friends and neighbors, and I received all of the haircuts of my early years on a board across the arms of that barber chair.

I remember it as a complicated piece of machinery. It could rise up or down with pressure on a lever near its base, operated with the barber's foot. It could recline with pressure on another lever—

this was one I was reluctant to touch because none of us kids knew how to set it upright again and the discovery of it with its backrest and footrest spread out was a sure sign that we had been playing where we were forbidden to play. It could spin. This was its greatest attraction. I had no doubt been introduced to this feature early on by my teen-aged uncle Gene, who liked to entertain me with lots of physical activity. If one kid sat in the chair and gripped the arms, another kid or two could set it spinning, faster and faster until it seemed it might lift right off its base and twirl across the floor like a top. It was like a merry-go-round with a smaller circumference and more dizzying centrifugal force. The basement revolved madly in a blur around you and when it finally stopped you hurried to get out of the chair so you could heighten your disorientation by lurching drunkenly around the cellar floor until your equilibrium returned. It was also forbidden to play on, of course, and my grandfather would be livid with rage if he caught us at it or found out about it afterward. But it was a risk we couldn't seem to stop ourselves from taking.

*   *   *

For me the universe was narrowly circumscribed and at the center of it was my grandma's house. My grandfather, except when he was angry, tended to say little and to interact little with other people in the house. My grandma, by contrast, was always in motion, cooking, cleaning, laundering, bustling, getting things done. She was the one who made the decisions in the house, the one who my grandfather turned over his weekly paycheck to and who then made all the purchases, did all the shopping, paid all the bills. She would be the one in the basement washing clothes, running them through the wringer, hanging them out on the clotheslines in the long back yard. She would be the one baking cookies in the time between making breakfast, lunch, and supper, long rows of chocolate chip cookies cooling on waxed paper on the counters and kitchen table, thick pans of dark fudge solidifying on top of the icebox. She would be the one gossiping with my mother, who would be smoking at the kitchen table, or with her younger sister, Josie (short for Josephine). She would be the one to arrange the visits to see her older sister Frances in Lowertown or her younger sister Florence half way to Buffalo or Josie and her husband Leo across town or her brother Joe and his wife Margaret a few blocks away from where we lived. There were always relatives and neighbors and friends dropping in, sharing the treasures of the cookie jar and the fudge tin, the endlessly percolating coffee pot, the ashtrays in the kitchen or, less often, the heavily upholstered chairs and couch in the living room. I don't remember anyone using the couches on the front porch, though it must have been pleasant enough to sit out there. Perhaps it was too far away from the action.

My daily universe was considerably more manageable. The center was the house at 281, with its small front yard and the large old oak in the front yard, low and easy to climb into and clamber around in, its long back yard with the rise at the end of it, all fenced in and good for running, an empty field across the street and Willow Park beyond it, with its wading pool, its swings and teeter-totters and merry-go-rounds and monkey bars, its ice-skating rink a long grassy depression in the ground through the warm months, its cannon at the corner, so perfect to shimmy out on and, if you were brave and bigger than I was, to hang from and drop to the ground. I must have played often with Bobby Hall and his older brother, Jimmy, who lived next door; they had a dog named Whitey, who in later years I thought of when I saw Mountie films featuring Chinook, the Wonder Dog. The Steiners lived across the street, in the house we would later buy, and Billy, whose age was between Bobby and Jimmy, was someone else I played with, though only Bobby and I were close enough in age to have very much in common.

It seems to me now, looking back and trying to recover those lost years, that from early on I felt like a Linderman or a Budnack, like a member of my mother's family, more than like a Root. In-laws always seemed to be accepted on sufferance, to not entirely fit in. Because I was already three by the time my father came home from the war and because we stayed in that house of my grandparents until I was in first or second grade, I was closer to my grandmother and her youngest son, my uncle Gene, than to anyone else, maybe even closer than I was to my mother. Certainly my grandma's house is one location I have no trouble traveling across time to revisit. I still know how it felt to live there.

49

UNCLE

IMAGES

In photographs my mother took in my early childhood, I often appear with my uncle, her youngest brother. He was fourteen when I was born into my grandparents' house, where my mother lived while my father served in the Marines. I was eight and a half months old in a picture where we both wear tee shirts bearing the words "U. S. Marines" and an image of the Marine emblem. The shirt drapes me to the ground, and I squint under a skewed baseball cap. In baggy khakis and sneakers, my uncle stands behind me, holding me upright, his arms lean but muscular and tanned, his light brown hair falling across his forehead as he looks down at me. In another photo I am in diaper and tee shirt, bare arms and legs, all blurry concentrated motion in the foreground while in the background he laughs at my efforts to walk. I am ten months old in a picture where he leans toward my high chair in my grandparents' kitchen as I offer him a piece of my food; I am a year and eight months old in the photo where he is on his hands and knees in the back yard and I sit unsteadily in the saddle on his back.

In a picture taken when I am three, my uncle hangs from a limb of the old tree in the front yard, exposing a gaping hole under the arm of his sweater, his legs wrapped around me and holding me off the ground. I wear a wool snowsuit and hood and hang nearly upside down, hand almost touching the ground. My mother's shadow in the foreground reveals her as the photographer, bent over the camera with the viewfinder on the top. Her shadow, the shadow of the tree on the lawn, tell me the picture was taken in late afternoon; the bare limbs tell me it is winter; the snowsuit, which I wear in other photos, tells me when it was taken. These photographs fill in for memory, and they remind me of the bond between my uncle and me.

What is clear in such photographs is his youthful strength and energy, his vitality, his persistent physicality. Most of the photographs he appears in show him in motion, here wrestling with my father, here dancing with my grandmother, here not sitting astride a horse but standing on the saddle, as if riding were not active enough. Even in posed photographs, where he simply stands beside others, he seems poised to move. He is the one who seems to be talking through the pose, making others laugh, commenting sardonically, lightening the occasion. Keeping still seemed to require too much effort.

For years I was the only child to enjoy my uncle's attention. He seemed determined to keep me laughing, to keep me in motion, to teach me how to be physical. I would be tossed in the air, balanced sitting on one of his hands or made to stand on his feet while he lay on the floor and slowly straightened his legs, challenging my balance. Children were always the fliers, he the catcher, in a one-ring circus he set up wherever he went. He promoted wrestling, was always the one to take on half a dozen preschoolers, tossing them aside and rolling them across the rug or onto the sofa, encouraging rough and tumble and toughing out injuries in the course of play and getting back into the action instead of sitting on the sidelines whimpering. I recall the lightness of my body, the sensation of flying through the air or being balanced giddily overhead; I recall my uncle's strength and control of the most seemingly haphazard and headlong movements.

He could walk on his hands the length and breadth of the house, moving erect but upside down from the living room to the kitchen and back, climbing the first three stairs to the landing and coming back down, at least once making it all the way upstairs. He trained me early in headstands, though I never was strong enough or balanced enough for handstands. He also made me practice dive-rolls, of which he was a master. The house, the yard were only local gymnasiums for him, and he would set up the hassock in the living room for me to dive over, flying straight across it, then tucking under, landing on my hands and shoulders and rolling out of it so I could come up onto my feet and run. He seemed unable to pass through a doorway without reaching up to grasp the molding and chin himself. In the yard he would jump from the garage roof, swing and drop from tree limbs, vault fences, and, as I grew older, encourage me and other neighborhood kids to do the same. It was like living with an acrobat.

I was the first born of my generation, the oldest grandchild, the one who lived the longest with my uncle; I became the one most given to climbing trees and leaping off roofs and throwing myself unexpectedly into a headstand. In the years to come, when families gathered at my grandparents' houses, I was also the one who wrestled with the younger kids, let them dog pile on me, tried balancing them on my feet and hands, roughhoused with them until I was tired and sweaty or until they tired of injury and defeat. Somehow I had come into my uncle's role on those occasions, although in every other way I had little connection with the lives of the younger siblings, nieces and nephews, and I lacked his agility and grace and strength.

When my father came back from the war, we met as strangers. We wouldn't really connect for decades. Perhaps what those images of me with my uncle also show is my father's absence. In a sense my uncle had been his surrogate and, even after my father's return, that's what he continued to be.

BABYSAT

After my uncle married his first wife, they moved to Lockport and for a time lived in a duplex apartment on the same street my parents and grandparents did. He had met her in Charleston, South Carolina, where he had been stationed in the navy. She spoke with a thick southern accent; she and my uncle had in common a penchant for smoking, drinking, dancing, and joking. She had a wide smile and a fierce gaze and a long stride; he tended to move with a sailor's rolling gait and the coiled alertness of a boxer. They were two young, vibrant, lively people. They laughed a lot, kidded one another and his brothers and sister and their friends, and often seemed ready for a party.

Occasionally they babysat me, though I'm uncertain how that came about with my grandparents living across the street from my parents, in a house I'd lived in with my mother the first years of my life and still visited daily, or where my younger sister and brother might have been while I was with my uncle and aunt. Their duplex was within easy walking distance of where we lived, just a little way up from the corner grocery, on the other side of the street, close enough for me to walk to on my own on occasion. I can foggily envision the arrangement of their living room, have a blurry image of the space they occupied, though no true details come to me. Just as foggily I suspect that my mother or my grandparents would come for me rather than make me spend the night.

One night, when my uncle and aunt were watching me, they took me with them to a downtown bar next to the Hotel Lox-Plaza, on the north side of the Big Bridge. It must have been summer, because it was warm, and it must have been late, because I remember it being dark outside.

They felt comfortable in bars—over the years to come I would follow him into a variety of taverns and, even in saloons he'd never been in before, my uncle walked in with the confidence and ease of a regular—and they moved through this one, local and familiar, deftly and cheerfully. I vaguely remember the layout of the bar, the way it deepened the further in we went, the round tables along one wall, the crowd of people, the noise level from the talk, the laughter, the clatter of bottles and glasses, the big band music on the large Wurlitzer jukebox, the open space where people danced.

My uncle and aunt were good dancers, he quick-footed, athletic, and agile, she long-legged, perpetually tanned, and lithe. It's easy for me to remember his laughter, her laughter, the fierce physicality each had. I wouldn't have known about earthy sensuality then, but, watching them, I may have suspected that it existed, even if I couldn't put a name to what they exuded.

It was late enough that people had been drinking for a while and my uncle and aunt drifted around the bar, briefly together but mostly separately, one of them remaining with me while I sipped root beer at their table and watched their cigarettes burn down in the ashtray amidst a pile of butts.

Then a woman got too close to my uncle and my aunt's eyes flared. I barely saw what she was looking at before she was away from the table and across the room. Her voice was angry, the other woman was defiant, one of them pushed or slapped the other one, and immediately my aunt was all over her. The crowd drew back and circled them as they fell together onto the floor. Then the onlookers closed off my view of the fight and suddenly my uncle was there beside me, gripping my arm and saying, "C'mon. I want you to wait for us outside."

As he steered me toward the street I protested, "What about her?"

My uncle smiled reassuringly. "Don't worry. Your aunt can take her." Then he positioned me against a wall and hurried back inside.

I stood alone on the street while the bar filled with people trying to see the fight, and I had no sense of what was happening inside. Soon my uncle and aunt came out, stepping quickly and eager to make us all scarce before the police arrived. In my memory she had a bruise near her left eye, but I may be wrong about that. She was still angry at the woman but had the presence of mind to start joking with me about the fight, suggesting we'd all had enough excitement for the evening. After we drove back to their place, my uncle advised me not to mention the night's events to my parents or grandparents—they might not be allowed to babysit me again if anyone else knew about the fight.

A few years later, after they'd had a daughter and a son together, while my uncle was at work, my aunt packed up her kids and their belongings and left. They were a long way gone on the road to South Carolina before he knew they weren't home. No one ever explained to me why she left—I had no idea then that marriages could end—though I think I knew intuitively that they had been a volatile mixture.

I never did tell anybody about the night in the bar. Instead, I haphazardly catalogued it in a file of things I knew about my uncle that others didn't know, things that I wouldn't try to understand.

A DRIVING LESSON

My uncle was energetic, intense, self-confident, optimistic about his passions. One of his passions was golf. In western New York, lake effect snows might sweep in from Lake Erie or Lake Ontario and bury the landscape anytime between November and May, but no matter how deeply blanketed the golf courses might be, my uncle began readying himself for the golfing season shortly after the first day of spring. He scorned any mention of meteorological happenstance, each year declaring that he would be golfing again come April 1st. He ignored comments from family and friends that snow would likely still be covering local courses, and he pretended—or behaved as if he believed—that winter would move out of the way when it was time for golfing to resume.

By the end of March he'd start checking out the county golf courses. Perhaps hoping to recruit his teenaged nephew to the game, one day he took me with him to look over conditions at a course on the east side of the county. The back road we traveled was narrow, bumpy, with no shoulder to speak of, and passed through barely inhabited farmland and fallow fields. It hadn't snowed recently, but the course was still mostly covered with dingy crystalline snow; open patches of fairway were few and scattered. We walked around some, my uncle estimating how soon the course would be snow-free and how quickly the groundskeepers could get it ready for play. He was cheered by his prospects. Then we began to retrace our way home, taking that back road again.

We were in my uncle's Mercury, the one with the winged messenger god on the hood. At some point, as my uncle joked and fantasized about getting on that golf course soon, I noticed him paying particular attention to the rear-view mirror. I could hear a car coming up behind us. Suddenly it roared past, two teenaged boys my age or older in the front seat. Once past us, the boy driving cut back into our lane too quickly. It was a thoughtless, careless maneuver, an immature driver misjudging distance and ignoring safety checks in his mirrors. Had his judgment been worse his rear end would have clipped the front of our car. In a few seconds his greater speed put more distance between us and I couldn't tell if he'd realized how close we'd been.

My uncle chuckled, said those boys needed a driving lesson, and pushed down on the accelerator. I felt myself thrust against my seatback, my feet instinctively braced against the floor. We gained on them rapidly. The teenager saw us coming and started to speed up but we closed in on their car until our front bumper was barely a foot or two away from their rear end. The boy stepped harder on the gas pedal and so did my uncle. We hurtled down the narrow two-lane, inches apart, at 60, 70, 80 miles an hour. The fields along the road were a blur, the boys in the car ahead glancing frantically around and behind them, my uncle smiling ferociously, my gaze alternately on him and on the car close ahead. I was terrified, speechless, certain that the four of us must crash.

Suddenly my uncle slowed slightly, whipped the Merc' into the passing lane, shot past the other car at nearly 90, then swerved close in front of them, rapidly decelerated, and smiled as they braked and fell behind us. He laughed, said how uncomfortable it must be to drive with your pants full, and thought they would pass other cars more politely from now on. He was happy. He'd done a kind of civic service, he thought, taught them a valuable lesson.

My pants were not full but I'd had a lesson too. We'd never met another vehicle on that road but I didn't believe we should have counted on that. Had someone been ahead of the boys or if the boy driving had panicked and swerved, there would have been deaths, perhaps the boys', perhaps a third party's, perhaps our own. I remembered the smile on my uncle's face, the terror on the boys' faces. Our lives had been at risk and I had none of my uncle's confidence that the risk was always in his control.

My uncle, on the other hand, was in good spirits all the way home. He was certain that in a week or so he'd be on this road again and he'd be playing golf by the first of April. He was very pleased by his prospects. For him, it had been a very good day.

MERCURY

I can still see the stretch of road where the accident happened, though I don't remember who took us to the scene or who I mean by "us." Perhaps one of his older brothers drove; perhaps my mother or grandfather or father; but I'm sure there were three or four of us. In my mind the black '49 Mercury is still upside down in the grass on the west side of a north-south running road in rural Niagara County, near Ransomville I think, though I could be wrong. The roof of the car is crushed, flattened, and there is virtually no space where the side windows had been. When it was upright, as I remember seeing it after the wrecker had hauled it off to the auto salvage, it appeared to have no roof at all. What had been roof was not merely flattened but pressed concave into the car's interior, which itself had been compressed lower. All the windows were gone and the front windshield frame was the only one that gave evidence of a window having been there. The front of the car was still intact—there'd been no collision; the car had flipped and spun and landed with its wheels in the air.

My uncle was by that time in the hospital and perhaps it was then, rather than before, that my mother said, "If he hadn't been thrown from the car, he'd have been killed." The patrol car that was the first on the scene—sheriff? state police?—at first could find no body though they peered into the car and all around it, backtracking along its trajectory, the trail it left rolling and sliding along the grass. Somehow someone looked on the opposite side of the road, on the east, and found him, bloody and unconscious. Someone may have told us that being drunk and being thrown from the car saved him—though being drunk was what caused the single car accident that threw him from the vehicle—because he didn't feel the impact—his body didn't resist it—which would have made his injuries worse. Lucky he was drunk. Lucky he was unconscious. Lucky he was driving so fast he was thrown from the car onto the opposite side of the road from where the Merc' landed. Even then all this struck me as spurious science and dubious good news.

My uncle was the only one in the family to drive a Mercury, the only one to own a non-GM vehicle. My father and my grandfather owned Chevrolets, another uncle a Pontiac. My grandfather and uncles all worked for Harrison Radiator, a division of General Motors, the company that dominated the economics of Lockport and much of Niagara County. But my uncle claimed the Mercury—a '49, I think—was a more substantial car—faster, most powerful, more responsive. He was also not above thumbing his nose at his employers by driving a Ford product into a GM employees' parking lot.

I knew almost nothing about cars, though this was a time in American life when people would tour the various showrooms each fall to see what all the new models looked like—the dealerships for Chevrolets, Pontiacs, Buicks, Oldsmobiles, and Cadillacs; Fords, Mercurys, and Lincolns; Dodges, Plymouths, DeSotos, and Chryslers; Packards and Studebakers; Nashes, Kaisers, and Hudsons. I thought well of the DeSoto and the Hudson because they were named for historic explorers (swashbucklers, in my mind), and I liked the Pontiac because it was named for an Indian chief and had an Indian profile as its hood ornament. I thought Chevy and Ford were boring, though occasionally it occurred to me that all the GM brands basically looked alike, as did all the Ford brands and all the Chrysler brands. But while others in my family would have selected their cars for utility or economy or brand-loyalty, my uncle selected his for sleekness and speed, and while their cars were sedately two-toned or light solid colors, his was jet-black.

Mercury, the wing-footed messenger of the gods, was on the hood ornament (I would have used only Mobil gasoline in it, based on its emblem of the flying red horse, which I assumed was Pegasus). Mercury symbolizes speed and agility. Looking at the squashed and damaged—totaled—wreck of my uncle's Mercury, I had no concept of irony.

But I did have an awareness that the appearance of resourceful invulnerability is not the same thing as real invulnerability. Perhaps the fact that he survived sailing across the road, through the air, and thudding into the tall grasses while his car rolled and crushed itself and scraped and slid to a halt on the other side of the road—perhaps that made him seem indestructible; perhaps when he was recovered, that's what he thought he must be. Did I really sense that, behind his continued bravado, he was aware of how close he had come to death—that much of the fierce defiance he displayed grew out of a determination not to be intimidated by the possibility of instantaneous destruction? Perhaps I only now feel as if I sensed it then. But whether he acknowledged to himself that he had not been in control of his destiny on that dark country road, I knew he hadn't been. I now believed that the worst consequences of his approach to life were not merely remotely possible but close to inevitable. From that moment on I couldn't shake my awareness of his vulnerability and, if I were aware of his, how could I help but feel my own even more?

GUNS

Where I occasionally hike these days, in a stretch of state forest, I often hear gunfire. Beyond the woods and a distant drumlin, a shooting club seems to have plenty of active members and a bottomless supply of bullets. It takes me about an hour or more to hike the three miles of that Ice Age Trail segment and no minutes pass when I experience woodland or prairie quiet unpunctuated by volleys of shots. I've never been to the club and can only imagine its layout, but it doesn't take long for the gunfire to trigger memories of my uncle's efforts to make me a marksman.

In the middle of my teens my uncle married his second wife, a woman somewhat older than he, with two teen-aged sons, one of them my age. For a time my step-cousin and I were constant companions and my uncle encouraged us both to pursue his passions. One of them was hunting. To get us used to handling firearms he would sometimes take us out to a quarry on the banks of the canal that passed through—indeed was the reason for the existence of—our town. There the high mounds of debris made a safe setting for target practice. Although I had a passion for western movies, books, and television shows, I wasn't eager to learn how to shoot, and gave my cousin more opportunities to handle my uncle's .22 than I took.

Guns were familiar to a good many of my uncle's friends. One day we visited a man who stabled horses and raised some livestock. My cousin and I stood near a pig pen which surrounded a dead tree in the middle of the barnyard. My uncle's friend had a .22 handy and to demonstrate its effectiveness casually shot a few starlings that had settled on the limbs of the tree. They fell into the muck below and the pigs scurried over to gobble them up. The friend told us the pigs liked the taste of starling. Since I thought pigs would eat just about anything, I wasn't sure that was true and didn't think their now snarfing up the dead birds counted as evidence.

Once, wandering in the woods with my uncle, he'd given my cousin and me chances to shoot at things. I was aware that the vision problems in my right eye made it hard for me to triangulate on locations; it reduced any accuracy I could hope for in throwing a baseball, for example, or aiming an arrow, and made it difficult to line up targets even with the help of sights on a rifle barrel. My cousin fired a couple of shots with success and then my uncle gave me the gun. He made adjustments to the way I held it, getting the butt against my shoulder just so, my hand on the fore stock just so, my head cocked just so in order to line up the sights. He pointed out a bird on a distant limb and told me to aim at it and squeeze the trigger. I could see the bird with my left eye but with my right eye I couldn't see even the front sight clearly. I pointed the rifle and pulled the trigger, and the bird toppled off the branch. My cousin ran over, picked it up, and congratulated me. "You bagged a robin."

I tried not to show how dismayed I felt. I'd thought I'd had no chance of shooting it and to discover it was a favorite songbird— not something anyone would really hunt, not something regarded as a pest, not something that might feed anyone or anything else— shamed me.

On another outing my uncle brought along a 12-gauge shotgun. This would have somewhat more of a kick to it, he warned us. My older step-cousin had no problems with it, and my younger step-cousin staggered at the discharge and rubbed his shoulder with an agonized look. Reluctantly, I raised the shotgun while everyone stepped back and, when I fired, the recoil knocked me off my feet. I sprawled backwards, the shotgun flying out of my hands, and landed hard on the stony ground. The whomp of my body hitting kept me from hearing the clatter of the weapon on the rocks. My uncle picked up the gun and dusted it off. He stood over me, watching me regain my breath, and told me I needed to change my stance.

The next time I fired a shotgun—it might have been the same gun or it might have been a different gauge—I stood firmly but didn't hold the weapon firmly enough. The recoil brought it forcefully into my nose and I staggered back, trying not to drop the gun again and suddenly aware that blood was gushing from my nostrils. For the rest of the outing I kept squeezing my nostrils together with a bloody handkerchief in my hand. It was the last time my uncle tried to teach me how to shoot.

My step-cousin continued to learn. One night, showing a girl cousin of his a shotgun in his bedroom, she pulled the trigger and shot a hole in the wall. The shot passed into my uncle's bedroom, above the bed where he and his wife were sleeping. I was glad not to have been there that night.

In time my uncle and his second wife divorced and she moved away and I lost track of her sons. My uncle moved back in with my grandparents. I never saw his guns again.

In between the time I graduated from high school and the time I went off, to everyone's surprise, including my own, to college, I lived with my grandparents. So did my uncle. In the evenings we watched television in the living room. It was a grand time for fans of westerns, which we both were, with shows every night: *Maverick* on Sundays, *Cheyenne* alternating with *Sugarfoot* and *Bronco* followed by *The Life and Legend of Wyatt Earp* and *The Rifleman* on Tuesdays, *Wagon Train* on Wednesdays, *Rawhide* on Fridays, *Have Gun, Will Travel* and *Gunsmoke* on Saturday nights. My uncle would be curled up in a chair near the picture window, sometimes meticulously trimming his fingernails and toenails, often commenting on the characters or the action.

My grandmother had a few favorite game shows that we also watched faithfully. On one, the host asked a gangly young man teamed with a pretty young woman if he liked her answer to a question; when the young man said, "I like everything about Marcia," she and he both blushed and we all laughed along with the television audience. My uncle remarked, "I bet he's got a whip on him like a stud horse," simultaneously outraging and delighting my grandmother and making me feel a bit more like one of my uncle's friends I'd met in bars he'd taken me to, where the talk was a little rougher at times.

My grandfather had given me his eight-year-old Chevy and I'd often run errands for or with my grandmother. At least once I'd taken her to look for my uncle, who hadn't come home the night before. Though she didn't say so, I suspected that she feared he'd been in another accident—he'd totaled two Mercuries driving alone and drunk in the middle of the night, and in at least one of the wrecks he'd been close to death from head injuries. We spotted his car in a parking lot in a neighboring small town and saw him coming out of a house. I never learned whose house it was, but I knew he liked women—after an all-nighter on the Tuscarora Indian Reservation, he told me cryptically: "Never take a chance on an Indian blanket"— and I think my grandmother suspected he might have been with a woman other than the young woman he'd been recently dating. His girlfriend had visited my grandparents' house and, because I liked her and my grandmother liked her, I didn't want to find out that she was right in her suspicions.

His girlfriend was someone he met at the factory who drove down to work from a northern suburb of Buffalo, about twenty miles away. Sometimes she'd come by for Sunday dinner or spend the evening watching television or playing games like *Sorry* or *Monopoly* with my uncle and me. She was quiet, a little shy, more earnest and thoughtful than his fiery first wife or his equally tough second wife, easy to shock and easy to embarrass.

One night, while we sat around and the grandparents were in bed, my uncle opened up a jug of hard cider he'd brought home from the house of a friend who fermented cider every winter. My uncle poured glasses for us all. His girlfriend sipped hers, my uncle drank his, and I treated mine as if it were simply the apple cider I was accustomed to. We sat on the living room floor around the game board, drinking and laughing, my uncle and me smoking, refilling our glasses. In time my uncle, who'd had some beers before he opened the cider, fell asleep and though I insisted on continuing the game, by now it was hard to keep track. At one point, his girlfriend cautioned me about my glowing cigarette and I thought it would be funny to throw it into the kitchen. I did and laughed as she scrambled after it. I didn't know why she wasn't amused.

The hangover I had the next day was agonizing and penetrating. If I'd been a smarter person, it would have been the last of my life. My uncle thought it was pretty funny and teased me by offering to fetch the jug for me—"Hair of the dog?"—mostly to see my reaction. I never drank hard cider again.

It may say something about what a nice person his girlfriend was that an evening that ended with her boyfriend asleep and snoring on the living room floor and his drunken teenaged nephew giggling goofily above a game board didn't make her end the relationship. She steered me to bed, helped him to bed, and drove home. Within a month or two she was pregnant and not long after that became my uncle's third wife, the most patient and adoring of them all. My uncle moved in with her across town and I had the guest room in my grandparents' house to myself.

I didn't know then that I would one day to go to college. I didn't have a job or a sense of the kind of life I might live if I were a grown-up, which it was dawning on me was what I was supposed to become. Living with my grandparents, like my uncle had, I was alone in their guest room. This was the place to which he retreated after divorces and crashes, the place where he licked his wounds and regrouped before setting out again into his own life. If I thought about it hard enough—and I tried not to—I knew that I had not retreated from anything but had simply hidden out from whatever life I would someday have to claim.

I could tell that it was time for me to come out of hiding, but, sitting in my uncle's place in his parents' home, I was aware that nothing I'd learned from him had taught me a way to do that.

Whenever I shovel snow I think of my uncle. In the past few weeks I've had occasion to think of him often and to observe, without much regret, how far I fall below the standard that he set for me in this area some decades ago.

In the winter of 1961, my uncle and I were both living with my grandparents. Their little ranch-style house was located on a large, open lot near the outskirts of town; their street, Nichols Street, had been a dead-end leading to open farmland only a few years before, and their house was one of several newly constructed when the street was extended into a through-road. While the older homes at the east end of the block were close together and fronted by tall thick trees, the new houses at the west end boasted only open spaces and scrawny saplings. Moreover, just to the west of our house, the street began to descend a sharply angled incline, making the buildings at the top of the hill even more exposed. When the winter wind would howl around the building, we would all be aware of the nakedness of our position.

That winter we got one of those classic lake-effect snowstorms that sweep in from Lake Erie and western Ontario and annually put the Buffalo area on the national nightly news. After a couple of hours of unrelenting snow, my uncle led me outside to clear the driveway for my grandfather's return from work.

The house had no sidewalk, only a concrete rectangle by the side door and a gravel drive the width of two cars. My uncle planned the shoveling like a military maneuver, intending not only to remove the snow but also to build a barrier against later drifting, all with the most efficient effort. He directed me to start in a certain place and to throw snow in a specific location while he would take up a different position and work to meet me in the middle. In effect, we were mounting a pincers operation against the blizzard.

At first the snow was light and fluffy, easy to toss aside, and the wind was light so that the snow fell straight down and didn't drift. In an hour the driveway was only dusted by fresh snowfall. However, the street remained untouched by city work crews and, as the wind began to rise, people returning from work were having difficulties getting into their driveways. By the time my grandfather's shift at the plant ended, my uncle and I had cleared the driveway twice and had begun to roam our end of the street helping others out of snowbanks.

Travelers' advisories were issued; my uncle's shift at the plant was cancelled; programming on the radio became a repetitious litany of closings and cancellations. The snow continued to fall, and the street before the house filled to the level of the yards on either side until all evidence of the road disappeared. Neighbors stopped shoveling, abandoned their cars, walks, and driveways to the snow, and barricaded themselves in their houses as if besieged. But we continued to work, as determined to keep our driveway clear as crusaders repelling infidels.

For the next two days we fought the snow, going out in shifts to shovel and clear, believing that short repeated forays would save us the agony of a massive battle when the blizzard abated. Our cars were snug in the garage, and in the moments when the wind lessened and the snow ceased, the driveway was visible as one long rectangle of gravel-flecked white, neatly laid-out between two high ridges of snow like a frozen-over harbor channel between icy piers. When the snow had hardened into crisp layers, my uncle had used his shovel to cut big blocks of frozen snow and pile them like fieldstones into a retaining wall against the blizzard. In two days the three of us constructed, on either side of the driveway, a wall forty feet long and higher than the eaves of the house.

A mason might have been proud of those walls—they were so straight and level that a surveyor might have set the lines to build them on. Sometime near the end of the siege I remember photographing my uncle and my grandfather standing before one of the walls, like soldiers at the gates of a successfully defended city or workmen at the completion of an architectural wonder. Surely no peasant working on the Great Wall of China or slave constructing the pyramids could have worked with such diligence and care, or felt as much the architect's pride as the workman's.

My uncle's mania for order, for precision, for planning, was the hallmark of the tasks he gave himself to do and the work he hired out to do; the rest of his life was more haphazard, and taught me by his example both the value of the rage for order and the need to be prudent about the places you vented it. The evidence of his own efforts showed me that men have to choose for themselves the places to find pride and pleasure in their building.

So, whenever I shovel snow, I think of my uncle, and if my snow removal is less conscientious—the borders of my walk seldom so straight, the snowbanks never built to last, my diligence in keeping the alley clear outmatched by my patience in waiting for city crews to do it—nonetheless I apply his example in the places where it matters most to me, and I always do my snow removal with good will, perhaps even with pride.

ACCIDENT

I stare at the headline in the newspaper clipping I have of the accident. "Baby Dead, Mother Hurt; Father Facing Charge." Succinct, terse, direct. I note the way the semi-colon interrupts the series, separating the baby and the mother from the father. The article tells us that the nine-month-old child died of a fractured skull, that the mother was in fair condition after being admitted to the hospital with "a broken nose, face lacerations and cuts and bruises," and the father, "who was driving the car, escaped with minor injuries." Escaped. He "escaped" while his wife and child did not.

The father was my uncle, the mother his third wife, the baby my cousin and their only child. The brother and sister the child is reported as being "survived by" were his half-siblings, children of my uncle's first marriage.

In the deputy's report the father recounted how "he had passed another car when he was blinded by bright headlights of an oncoming vehicle. He lost control of his auto which went into a skid." The car overturned and the deputy reported that "skidmarks ran for 323 feet and that the car was 60 feet from the road when it stopped," upside down on someone's lawn. At an arraignment the following morning, the father pleaded innocent to a charge of driving while impaired by alcohol and was released on $100 bail. I don't know whether, at his hearing a week later, anyone testified that this was the third car he had totaled and the only accident in which someone was with him when he crashed.

Certainly that was a fact that haunted me.

My uncle was thirty-three, his wife twenty-six, and my cousin nine-months old. Her pregnancy with him had precipitated the marriage and I had babysat him and played with him and been close to him throughout his short life. His death was nearly unbearable for all of us who had loved him.

I remember going to the junkyard to view the red Mercury with others in my family, including my sister and brother. I kept remembering the first wrecked Merc' and how this one wasn't as devastated, though the passenger side bore the brunt of the crash. The windows were broken, the front windshield gone. I remembered how lucky everyone said my uncle had been to have been thrown

71

from the car in that first accident. Surviving this one with "minor injuries" didn't seem quite so fortunate to me.

At the memorial service, before my cousin was buried in the children's section of St. Patrick's Cemetery, a priest who was called in to officiate performed the service largely by rote. He hadn't known my uncle or aunt or cousin or most of us in the room, and he concentrated on the mysterious ways God works in the world and urged us not to question them. I hadn't been a very good or very devout Catholic through most of my eighteen years, but my rage at the priest distanced me further from the church. I couldn't then—I can't now—imagine a good reason for any god to approve the death of a thriving, healthy, happy child. I felt my sister and brother bristling beside me, saw the anger in my mother's face.

Had it been "just an accident," some happenstance beyond anyone's control, we might have been more ready to ignore the priest and his preoccupation with approved ritual. But not all of us could keep from feeling conflicted about our loyalty to my uncle. My grandmother was angry at the other driver, the one who "blinded" my uncle, and no one wanted to argue in front of her that it was unimaginable that my uncle hadn't been drinking, that he hadn't been speeding, that he hadn't take a risk he shouldn't have taken. No one wanted to remind her of the other drunken accidents. And so we were angry at the priest and the other driver and the driver my uncle was trying to pass and the deputy who investigated the accident and the judge who arraigned him. Or we said nothing, and if we thought the priest would have been on more solid ground to assert that God had punished my uncle by taking away his son, we couldn't justify God's punishing the child's mother, whose fault had been loving my uncle, in the same way.

My brother and sister and I talk about our distance from the priest's view of the memorial service, whenever we remember my cousin's death. And it's my cousin's death, the loss of him, that we claim to remember. The memory comes back at every memorial service we attend, as if we're evaluating each priest or minister against the model that priest set. But I know I remember the accident itself, and the accidents before them, and my uncle's jovial intemperance in terms of speed and alcohol.

By now there have been other deaths, lots of them, deaths of grandparents and parents and their siblings and in-laws and cousins, deaths of relatives I barely knew in their generations. It might have been cancer or heart disease or some vague medical condition that took them, and once an aged alcoholic granduncle suffocated in a dingy hut somehow, but we children were often told it was simply "old age"—reaching a point in life where you just no longer have the wherewithal to stay alive. Death is normal; death is natural. We had to accept its inevitability for those of certain ages with certain health problems.

But my toddler cousin's death had not been normal or natural or inevitable; at that moment, in our extended family, he had been the very youngest of my generation, bright, healthy, happy. His death marked a turning point for some of us, most certainly for me. For over fifty years I have been sadder about the world than I was before he left it.

As deeply as I shared the anguish and relentless grief my aunt and my uncle felt, some portion of my sorrow grew from sensing the loss of my connection with my uncle. Perhaps I had known for a very long time that, no matter how close we had been, I had had no likelihood of carrying on many aspects of him. Probably the gap or gulf between us, unspoken and unacknowledged, had been as clear to him as it had been to me, indicated by my reluctance to master boxing, my ineptitude at marksmanship and athletics, my unwillingness to take risks. All along I tried not to make the unlikelihood of my achieving his kind of manliness apparent. And then there was the accident. I could keep quiet about my persistent sense of his responsibility for it, but I couldn't absolve him in my own mind.

Sometime in a future I had given no thought to I would have to become someone other than who I was now and I was sadly aware of how little I would end up resembling my uncle.

When I look at the photograph of my uncle and his second Mercury in our driveway—that's my Schwinn near the steps, the fastest vehicle I propelled myself in at the time—I try to sort out my feelings about his influence in my life, which was more or less constant from the time I was born until the time I went to college and became a different person than who I was before.

Although, if I think about it carefully, not everything was different about me.

Echoes of my life with my uncle sound unexpectedly from time to time, in little things, at odd moments. I am now a grandfather, a semi-retired English teacher, a man who takes exercise and yoga classes for senior citizens in order to keep in shape. Yet when my yoga instructor demonstrates a headstand—a move she expects none of us to imitate—I flash back to my childhood, when my uncle taught me headstands and walked around the house upside down on his hands. In junior high I was involved in a gymnastics show only once and my only trick was doing a headstand. My mother and my uncle were in the audience but before my performance, the coach decided not to include headstands. I was disappointed; I wanted to show my uncle how his example had paid off for me. Instead the highlight of the event for him ended up being his yelling "Yee-haw" from the sidelines during a country dance number. Still, I've sometimes shown my grandchildren my headstand, now executed with more care and less grace than I learned it.

I have been the horsie for my grandchildren, the bucking bronco, the wrestler on the floor and the relentless tickler, and sometimes the tumbler helping them to fly. And every time I am, I remember my uncle on the floor of my grandparents' living room and the rough burgundy sofa onto which I would be tossed; I remember being the oldest grandchild recruited to take my uncle's role in wrestling with much younger cousins. Once, several years ago, walking around a Boulder bookstore with reading glasses on, I missed the first step off the second floor and tumbled down the stairs, ending flat on my back on the broad wooden landing. When another customer rushed over and asked if I was alright, I said I needed to think about it. But I was, and recognized almost at once how I had rolled into the fall the way my uncle had made me practice, diving over the ottoman or over the backyard fence again and again. When I stood up, I was a little sore and a lot embarrassed but still mobile and grateful to my uncle's training.

Everyone in my family read, though none of them, myself included as a child, read anything that would predict that I would one day teach literature and become a writer. In my grandmother's house, while he and I and my mother lived there, my uncle would head upstairs to the bathroom, announcing, "I'll be in the library." The shelf opposite the toilet always held copies of *Field and Stream, Argosy, Police Gazette,* one or two other sports or men's magazines, and maybe some copies of *Modern Romance* and *True Love,* my mother's or grandmother's magazines. None interested me very much, but the habit of taking reading to the bathroom—now an issue of *The New Yorker* or *The New York Times Book Review*—has stayed with me all my life.

At family events, weddings and reunions, wherever there was a dance floor, my uncle would be on it, spry, lively, agile, often jitterbugging with my mother. When my mother showed me some dance steps, I consciously imitated my uncle's dexterity. It was only after I went to college that I let myself loose as a dancer, enjoying whatever partner joined me and whatever dance steps they taught me how to do. Sometimes I remembered my uncle and his first wife dancing in that hometown bar.

But I have to admit to having been conflicted about my uncle's influence, circumspectly resistant to some of the ways he hoped to help me become a man. I never did well in the boxing ring he set up in my grandparents' garage, never handled a gun again after a shotgun's recoil gave me a bloody nose, am still not much of a swimmer since the time he tried to teach me with the sink-or-swim method at a local beach. Once, when some younger driver switching lanes cut me off and then roared ahead of me, I stomped my foot on the gas pedal and started after him. My wife, suddenly alarmed, asked, "What are you doing?" My first thought was to say, "I think he needs a driving lesson," but instead I answered, easing off on the accelerator, "Driving like my uncle."

I wonder what mechanism we have inside us—or do I just mean, inside me?—that determines what influences stay with you and what drops away. How did I, who was so distant from my own father, so close to my uncle, over the years become more like my father, morose and responsible, and less like my uncle, irrepressible and impulsive? How much of my uncle's playfulness, exuberance, rebelliousness, is still active inside me, tempering timidity, rigidity, propriety?

No one told me until long after he was buried that my uncle had died. I missed his funeral and, when I learned of his death, remembered at once one of the last times I saw him, at my grandmother's funeral. When he heard me call my teenage son "Honey," he punched me in the arm and shook his head. That was the last lesson he tried to teach me. I smiled and ignored it, though I recognized at once the uncle I had always known.

Interlude: 2 Chestnut Street

no. 2 chestnut St, Cooperstown. N.Y.

2 Chestnut Street, Cooperstown, New York, was the house built for the lawyer Horace Lathrop in the early 1800s. It was the home of his son, the physician Horace Lathrop, and of the physician's daughter, Mary Lathrop. The physician lived in it all his life and died in it; his daughter lived in it all her life as well, and was married to Charles W. G. Ross in it. Their daughters, the twins Delia and Helen, Jean, and Flora Ellison, who died in childhood, were born and grew up in it. Delia, or Betsy, my grandmother, married my grandfather, Arthur Root, in it. After Betsy's father died, her mother continued to live in the house with Helen and Jean until she died in 1939; the daughters eventually moved into a small house around the corner on Lake Street. But for many years this was the house that my grandmother and grandfather brought their children back to visit in Cooperstown.

It seems unlikely that no one told me about this house, in the years that my family visited my father's maiden aunts in Cooperstown, but if they did I had forgotten and the discovery of the house late in my life was strangely moving to me.

Perhaps it goes back to Julian Barnes's question about what we carry on from one generation to another and, in this case, at least, how we can carry on anything from generations before us that we never knew. By the time my father and his sister, my aunt Fran, were born, their grandfather Ross was dead, and even Art Jr., the oldest child, had barely come into the world before C. W. G. Ross left it, but their grandmother Ross was there in that family home until they were nearly adults. It had a centering influence on them.

Aunt Fran has written, "I have fond memories of my Grandmother Ross's house. It was the one constant in my childhood, we moved around so much. But we always managed to visit Cooperstown once or twice a year." Her father's parents, Winfield Scott and Evalina Root, lived a few blocks away, on Nelson Avenue, but their house "did not have any particular family history attached to it." The Roots hadn't always lived in Cooperstown, and during the Depression they sold that house and came to live in Lockport with Arthur and his family. So the solid link to family history was always 2 Chestnut Street.

Fran once stayed in the house when it became for a time a bed and breakfast inn. Her tour of it brought back memories, the way revisiting a familiar site will do. She sees the "old one-car garage . . . in the back corner of the lot" and remembers how it was "too small to get our car in when we visited." She notes that "the somewhat formal flower gardens are gone" and recalls how "Aunt Helen cut fresh flowers for the house every day." In downstairs rooms that have shifted their purposes she remembers "comfortable chairs near the fireplace" and a piano in the parlor, which "still has the long down-to-the-floor windows looking out on to the side porch." She remembers the large kitchen with "a huge old coal stove" and "Aunt Jean ironing with the old sad irons, heated on the stove." She remembers the basement, "dirt floor mostly, old coal bin, and fruit cellar. It even smelled the same." She remembers the staircase "with banisters well-suited for children to slide down" and the stained glass window that is still on the first landing. On the second floor, her grandmother and Aunt Helen shared "a sort of master suite . . . two open rooms" and Aunt Jean had a separate bedroom. Fran often slept in another bedroom when the family came to visit and Art had a bedroom in the attic. "The attic was a place to play in my childhood," she writes, "a big empty space inhabited by bats, which I avoided. And another big storage space with old trunks, a wheelchair, and lots of interesting stuff to play with or peek into."

My aunt's memories open up a new world to me, or perhaps simply expand the world of my own memories. The house was no longer in the family when I went to Cooperstown as a child and yet somehow I feel connected to it and to the people who inhabited it. Place can have that effect, as if the memories have been preserved in the air around it, transmittable not only to those who lived the memories but also to those who only have vague knowledge about the memories. As I try to recover my own memories I sometimes try to occupy the spaces I've inhabited in the past, and usually the act conjures something up. With this house the conjuring comes vicariously but no less forcefully.

*   *   *

Cooperstown was something like a mythic family past for me. It was the town where my father was born, even though his parents lived in Syracuse at the time of his birth; his mother returned here to deliver both his brother Art in 1920 and him in 1921. It was the community in which my grandfather and my grandmother had come of age, graduated from high school, courted and married. It was the town my father continually returned to visit, bringing his children along.

By the time I knew it the family past was largely over. My paternal great-grandfather had died on the farm of a nephew in rural Otsego County in 1950. By then his sons had scattered, one to Colorado, one to Germany, my grandfather to the northwestern corner of New York State, and his only daughter was a Presbyterian missionary in Korea who rarely returned stateside. My father's maiden aunts, Helen and Jean, lived together in a small house a few doors down from the large house in which they had all grown up.

I remember Cooperstown only as a town centered around that small pink one-story house on Lake Street. It was a town of statues. Around the corner was the statue of a World War I infantryman astride a large boulder, his rifle in his hands, his legs spread apart, as if ready for battle. We knew that statue because Grandpa Root's name was one of those inscribed on the bronze plaque below the soldier, names of those from Cooperstown who served in the United States Expeditionary Forces. In the park down by the lake was the statue of an Indian hunter and his dog, facing Lake Otsego, the Glimmerglass. This was a statue more in the spirit of the place for us, since everyone called it "Leatherstocking and His Dog" and somehow tied it to the Leatherstocking novels of James Fenimore Cooper, son of the founder of the town. The statue supposedly caught the Indian on the watch up the length of the lake, perhaps for the return of the Deerslayer. Each time we stood below the statue I tried to imagine for a moment the park empty of people, the lake devoid of powerboats, and the Glimmerglass mirroring the unbroken forest along its shores and blue sky above it, the surface smooth but about to be broken by the appearance of the Deerslayer pursued in his canoe by hostile warriors while his friend Chingachgook watched and waited.

And there was the Cooper statue too, the seated figure of the man who had created the Leatherstocking saga, the very image of a confident, accomplished, accessible author. The first books I remember receiving as gifts were hardbound copies of *The Deerslayer* and *The Last of the Mohicans,* the Scribner's editions with the N. C. Wyeth illustrations, given to me by Aunts Helen and Jean. For a very long time I thought that we were somehow related to James Fenimore Cooper. He was the first author I regarded with any veneration, as much for my mistaken sense of him as my own ancestor as for his creation of Natty Bumppo. At some point I must have suggested that we were descendants of James Fenimore Cooper, a misconception spurred by family origins in Cooper's Town and the Cooper books presented almost as heirlooms rather than as birthday gifts, and my father scornfully straightened me out. It was an early disappointment, this loss of connection to a literary eminence, and I felt discouraged by the discovery.

The Cooperstown I was interested in was Natty Bumppo's Cooperstown. Each time we visited—it seems to me it was always in summer—my father would take us out to Natty Bumppo's cave, a place we would hike to in the woods. In Cooperstown Nathaniel Bumppo, also called the Deerslayer, Hawkeye, the Pathfinder, *la longue carbine,* took on the mantle of historical existence, as Tom and Huck and Becky Thatcher do in Hannibal, Missouri. I seemed to feel his presence in Cooperstown, though I knew that the cave was mostly a place that Dad and his brother had liked to play when they had come here as children. When we occasionally would get out on the lake in a boat, it was the historical romance connected with the lake rather than the scenic beauty or the stylishness of the homes and vacation cottages and resorts along its shores that captured my imagination. For me it was always the Glimmerglass, the setting of the adventures in *The Deerslayer*, and my desire was always to depopulate its shores and thicken its forests as they were in the Wyeth pictures.

I liked the house of Aunt Jean and Aunt Helen for its neat compactness, its closeness to the lake, and its crammed bookcases. I must have known then that Helen was my grandmother's twin, and I recall examining the photographs of the three sisters on the bookshelves, trying to locate my grandmother in Helen, and Helen in my grandmother. I remember the affection our great-aunts had for us, especially Helen, and I knew from a very early age that some portion of that affection came to us as a gift on my grandmother's behalf. We were their dead sister's grandchildren, the offspring of her second son, and I seemed to feel not only a sense of obligation in the fondness but also an accompanying sense of loss.

Cooperstown was a town of public ghosts, whose memorials were everywhere—in the Baseball Hall of Fame, at the Farmer's Museum, at the Cooper Memorial—but it was also a town of family phantoms as well, ones I have learned about very late in life. I look now at the photo of the house at 2 Chestnut Street and think about the lives that began there and that ended there that I never really knew about. I always associated the town with a colorful and adventurous past, and my father's family as one somehow connected with history. It was harder for me to see this family, this history, as somehow my own, and it's only now that I'm beginning to recognize that it was.

GRANDMOTHER

PORTRAIT

What do we see when we look at a photographic portrait? Knowing that the person in the portrait has posed for the photographer and that the picture we see is probably only one of several alternate photographs taken that day, how much can we assume the person in the portrait has been revealed to herself or to anyone else by her image? This is, I suppose, the challenge we face with any portrait hung in a museum, though there we are distracted by our attention to the artist's technique and aesthetic decisions or perhaps comparisons with other artists of that era. In portraits of the prominent by contemporary photographers, we likely respond to the persona the subject chose to display or the photographer chose to illustrate.

But most of us have had our portraits taken for one sort of commemorative occasion or another: the school yearbook, graduation, wedding, employer's promotional event. We usually have a portfolio to look through, a chance to choose the photo we hope best represents ourselves the way we want to be seen by whoever views the image. Often the photos have been retouched at the photographer's studio, blemishes deleted, colors heightened or subdued, background cropped to increase or decrease contrast. If we hold up the final portrait, place it on our shoulder, and face ourselves in the bedroom or bathroom mirror, how often does the face of the living subject replicate exactly the face preserved in the photo? How well does the commemorated *you* record the living *you*? How well, I wonder, would the living face of the woman in the portrait that hung in our living room all the years I was growing up have resembled her photographic image?

It's a question I haven't been able to stop asking for some time now.

The woman in the portrait is my grandmother, Delia Lathrop Ross Root. Her middle name recorded her mother's lineage and became both my father's middle name and my own. Her nickname was Betsy, because she was a Ross by birth, and it stuck with her all her life. Her portrait hung on our living room wall, near a similarly large portrait of my mother in her wedding gown; eventually, in the sorting out of items after the death of my parents, it came to me. By that time my grandmother had been dead for over fifty years. She died the day after my fifth birthday.

I would like to think that, in those five years between my birth and her death, we spent time together. We lived, after all, in the same city, her house a five-minute drive from where my mother and I lived with my maternal grandparents while my father was away at war. Surely on occasions such as my second Christmas, when he was home on leave, my parents would have visited my father's parents with me in tow. And after the war two years passed between my father's return and my grandmother's death when he might have taken me to see her. But I have no memory of that happening. Increasingly I find myself haunted by the absence of such a memory.

I am one of those family members who tend to hang on to old notes and letters and scrapbooks and albums. I didn't stay much in touch with my father's side of the family until after my father's death, when I reconnected with my father's sister and some of her children. One of them, my cousin Janet, had a similar tendency to hoard old photos, and on a visit at her home in Kansas she showed me a treasure trove of images. Here were pictures of my father's childhood and photos across the span of my grandmother's life. The only picture of her I had ever seen was that portrait in our living room. I duplicated as many of Janet's photos as I could, fascinated at the chance to have family history open up to me in this visual way.

But there was more. My cousin and my aunt shared photocopies of columns my grandmother had written in 1937 for a

Buffalo, New York newspaper. My aunt told me that my grandmother had once written an autobiography, later destroyed, and a portion of a novel, which she let me copy. Now I had images of my grandmother and texts she had written. I had never known— or never remembered— how my grandmother had died, but now I learned that she had struggled against asthma all her adult life and that she had died because of it. My wife, who herself has asthma, told me that she could see traces of it in my grandmother's face in that portrait, the last photograph taken of her before her death. As someone fascinated by synchronicity, I was stunned to realize that I had married a woman who suffered from the same illness that had killed my grandmother. The convergences were becoming overwhelming.

In time I tracked down all of my grandmother's columns and assembled a complete set of the feature from the *Buffalo Courier-Express,* deciding to publish it so that all of her surviving descendants and any of their descendants to follow might have access to it. I wanted them to be able to hear her voice when they read her. I wrote my own family memoir, learning as I did of the influence she had been on my father and, consequently, all unknown, an influence on me.

Yet, as I wrote the introduction to *How to Develop Your Personality*, I was aware that I really didn't know Betsy Root as well as I wanted to. Each day I would pass a younger portrait of her on my bookshelf and recall at once the formal portrait I had always known and wonder how to connect the two. If these were the same person, what did they have in common across the span of decades?

And so I return to Betsy's portraits, her snapshots, her columns, her unfinished novel, the single note I have in her own handwriting that she sent to my mother before my parents were married. Who do I see when I see those images? Who do I hear in the voice(s) of her prose? How can all these artifacts and literary remains help me come to know my grandmother? Who will I finally see in her portrait?

I have two early photographs of the Ross sisters from the end of the 19th Century and the beginning of the 20th. The earliest shows three girls, the twins Delia and Helen, born in 1895, on either side of Jean, born in 1898 and probably less than a year old when the photograph was taken. The woman behind them, with Jean on her lap, looks down toward the top of the blonde girl's head. I've enlarged the photo as much as I can on my laptop to see if her eyes are open and still can't be certain. I think she must be their mother, Mary Lathrop Ross, but I don't know for sure. The second photograph pictures all four daughters of Charles and Mary Ross. Delia and Helen must be around five years old here, Jean around three. The youngest, Flora Ellison, was born in 1900 and died within a year after it was taken.

I smile at the look of incredulity on infant Jean's face in the earlier photo, her eyes alight with curiosity and wonder. In the later photo I'm delighted by Flora's bright, eager gaze at someone, perhaps her mother, behind the photographer. She is at that open, guileless stage of her infancy. Her sisters keep a firm grip on her. In both pictures the older girls seem to take the experience more seriously. I slowly scan their faces, wondering if the expressions captured in the photograph say anything about their personalities.

Jean, standing behind the others in the later picture, seems the most concerned about the enterprise, the most uncertain about how she should behave. In a sense her expression reinforces the sense of her in the earlier picture, here her gaze more cautious, more deferential. Helen, the light-haired twin, shows some concern in the first photo, a tight, attentive smile in the second. Perhaps she tends to worry more about approval than her sister does.

Delia, the dark-haired twin, who will become my grandmother in some forty years, is the child I concentrate on most. In the earlier photo, her gaze is the most direct, the most intense, the least intimidated. She stares at the camera head on and leans on her mother's right leg with her left arm. I sense a seriousness about her. In the later photo the baby sits on her lap and hers is the arm that holds the child in place. Her tight-lipped expression and straightforward gaze suggest determination, as if having been assigned the job of holding on to the baby, she is working harder at it than the job requires.

I keep both images up on my computer screen, enlarging them and centering Delia's face in each, leaning close to look into her eyes.

And there's the challenge and the promise of photography: the sense that the preserved image records individuals at vital stages of their lives. Searching for computer copies of my grandmother's images I've blundered into folders with dated photos of my grandchildren and find myself idly clicking them to watch the transformations as they occur across time. There's my granddaughter posing as a ballerina at five and here she is at twelve on-stage at a performance of her dance class. There's my grandson at one and a half laughing in the carrier on his father's back and here he is at ten concentrating on a chess match against his grandmother. I've been present at so many of the stages of their young lives and seen them grow into the people they are now and, for a little while longer at least, will observe the people they grow into. I think I know who they are. If I line up the images I have of them I observe the physical transformations and sense the transformations in personality that accompanied them because I've known them at so many of the moments the images record. Of course the linkage has gaps but as yet none are so unbridgeable that they seem like strangers to me.

And now I can assemble a similar sequence of images in my grandmother's life, though the gaps in time are considerably wider in my collection than those in my grandchildren's chains. That child in the photo with her sisters will become the young woman in later photographs, the wife and mother in even later photographs, the woman in formal portraits closer to the end of her life. To someone who knew her through all those stages—both Helen and Jean lived at least a decade longer; my grandfather, her husband, survived her by nearly fifteen years—the images are reminders of who she was at each stage. That's the promise of the images. The challenge of them is in the likelihood of transmitting her serial identities to someone who only has the images to go on.

DELIA AT GLIMMERGLASS

I've cropped the photo some—taken out tree limbs that fill the upper third of the image—to emphasize her more, give less attention to the background and more to the figure at the center of it. The outfit is rather simple: a white blouse, a black skirt and boots, a white hat in her hands. She stands upright, feet together, hands together on the brim of the hat, gaze fixed on the photographer. That gaze: forthright, intent, almost stern. She gives nothing away, offers no sense of her mood at the moment or her feelings about the place where she stands or the person behind the camera. On the white border of the photograph, in ink that resists bonding with the surface, someone has written with a sprawling hand, "Delia at Glimmerglass."

From the first time I saw the photo, the caption has held my attention almost as much as the figure of the young woman it records. I always think of her as "Betsy," seldom refer to her as "Grandmother," and never as "Grandma" or "Gram," the names I use for my mother's mother—Anna Linderman had a constant physical presence in my life, Betsy none at all. But I've known that Betsy's given name was Delia, named for her maternal grandmother, Delia Ann Paddock Lathrop. At least one aspect of trying to "carry on" past generations is inserting family names into those of new generations. Her parents' first child, Horace Lathrop

Ross, was named after both Betsy's grandfather and great-grandfather and died in infancy, before Delia Lathrop Ross and her twin, Helen Appleton Ross, were born; their sister Jean got Paddock for a middle name. Perhaps the nickname Betsy came later in Delia's life or was never used by her parents, at least not by whoever wrote the caption.

What's in a name? "Delia," to my ear, evokes dignity, a certain refinement or reserve; she is addressed in sonnets by Samuel Daniel, in poems by William Cowper and Henry Wadsworth Longfellow, and in classical literature. "Betsy" is casual, an affectionate replacement for a more formal name; heroines with that name are rambunctious, perky, animated, determinedly individual. If the historical flag maker had been named "Elizabeth Ross," my grandmother would likely have stayed "Delia." I admit each time I see this photograph I think of the young woman there as Delia.

The location in the caption is evocative for me as well. The Glimmerglass is the name for Otsego Lake in *The Deerslayer,* a tale set in the wilderness here around 1740. Today Glimmerglass State Park borders the northeastern shore of the lake and the Glimmerglass Opera is located on the northwest corner. The Village of Cooperstown occupies the southern end, where the Susquehanna River flows out of the lake. When my family drove from Lockport to Cooperstown in our station wagon, crossing from western New York to south central New York on state highways, mostly ignoring the brand-new New York State Thruway, the last eight or nine miles would take us south near the western shore of the lake. I would perk up at signs evoking sites named for James Fenimore Cooper's sagas—Leatherstocking Falls, Leatherstocking Golf Course, Glimmerglass Road, Fenimore Art Museum—and hope that sometime in our visit we would wander around the Farmer's Museum or get another chance to hike to Natty Bumppo's Cave, while my brother looked forward to Doubleday Field and the National Baseball Hall of Fame. The word "Glimmerglass" can immediately start those family memories, along with images of N. C. Wyeth's covers for Cooper's books, roiling in my mind.

If I think of all those things we saw and did on our trips back to my father's roots (yes, I recognize the play on words but can't avoid it; the present readily uproots the past unless we commit ourselves to preserving it), I have to acknowledge that the

Cooperstown we visited and the Glimmerglass we longed for were not the village and the lake that Delia knew, and she did not know the village and the lake of James Fenimore Cooper's experience or imagination. But the Glimmerglass beyond the trees behind Delia was the scene of the Root family outings, so fondly remembered by my grandfather's sister, those days sailing with shredded wheat boxes full of picnic meals. Perhaps the Roots were out there the day this photograph of Delia was taken; there's no way to know. The picture of Delia at the Glimmerglass doesn't help me bridge the gap— I shouldn't expect it to— and I'll never know who took it. Was she on an outing with her sisters? Was she with friends? Was she with a beau, perhaps even Arthur Root? It's simply a solitary image and I have no way to add further context to it.

The look on Delia's face, her almost willful, perhaps determined refusal to give her features expression, together with her upright stance and smallness against the background of the image, keeps me at a distance. And yet it locates her for me in time and place. I don't recognize the exact spot where she stands but I know I've stood in such a space along that shoreline. I too have felt a connection with the Glimmerglass.

For the time I gaze at the picture, Cooperstown and the lake are not simply sites of my father's history and of remote literary associations. They are also mine and for an ever so brief moment I share them with Betsy.

BETSY

How old was she in this portrait? I can't tell and the image had no date on it. I'm guessing late teens. She was perhaps three and a half decades younger than she was in the portrait I'm most familiar with. The photographer has given her an ethereal air—that shaded, barely solid background, the dissolving of her clothing into the white of the paper, the way her collar covers her shoulders almost as if she were wearing devotional robes. It's a precise image, giving detail to the upsweep of her hair, the shadows around her neck, the intensity of her gaze.

It's the gaze that captures me, that led me to copy the photo and frame it and place on my bookshelves along with other family pictures. Hers is the only image there of someone I have no recollection of ever having met, and yet hers is the most gripping of them all.

In all the time her last portrait hung on my family's living room wall, my siblings and I hardly knew what to make of it. From time to time one of us would ask again who that lady in the picture was. In a portrait nearby, we recognized our mother, somewhat younger than she was in the flesh but not so many years removed from the woman we saw daily. But even when we were told—again—that the woman in the other picture was our grandmother, our father's mother, we had difficulty making the connection. We had only one grandmother, our mother's mother, and the image on the wall didn't resemble anyone we knew, not our father or his brother or his sister. We visited his siblings and their children often enough to know them all on sight and perceived no trace of her in them, of them in her.

But in this teen portrait of Betsy I saw my father's face in hers for the first time. More surprising, I see my own face in hers. I'm the one in my family who most resembles my father and gazing at Betsy in this photo I felt a sense of linkage I hadn't felt before. As the vanished woman in the living room portrait she was an enigma, but in the small teen portrait of her I seem to feel her presence.

This well could be a graduation photograph from 1914. The only artifacts we had of hers in our house were four individual plays by William Shakespeare and a copy of Edward Fitzgerald's translation of *The Rubaiyat of Omar Khayyam,* awarded to Delia L. Ross on April 10, 1914 as the Edward Clark Punctuality Prize. Two of the plays have her maiden name in them and speeches by Puck in *A Midsummer-Night's Dream* and Mercutio in *Romeo and Juliet* have been marked on their pages, as has the blinding of Gloucester scene in *King Lear—King John* is unmarked except for some of my sister's early attempts at lettering in the flyleaves. I still have all five volumes and I still wonder if those books suggest something about the personality of the young woman who possessed them first.

Look at the expression on her face, the intensity of her gaze, the brightness of her eyes—hazel eyes like my father's, like mine— the earnest set of her lips. There is confidence here, intelligence, determination. I enlarge the photo on my laptop, bring her features in closer, make them life-sized, make them beyond life-size. I can't help trying to match her gaze and find it hard to look away. I keep staring into her eyes and can't stop feeling that she is staring back into mine. As if she recognizes me. Is that the faintest glimmer of a knowing smile around her lips? Without my ever realizing it, have we been connected all along?

She must have seen me as an infant, as a child, in the five years between my birth and her death. Is there any part of that child still visible in my aged face or would she recognize my father's face in mine and know who I am? When I return to the portrait taken three and a half decades later, after years of asthmatic illness and not long before her death, will I see this young woman in my grandmother's face? If I had found the photos together without being told who the subjects were, would it be obvious to me that they were both the same person?

And yet they were. And yet they are. And no matter how altered in appearance the older Betsy might be from the young Betsy I look at here, surely the same personality, the same identity, will be there in either portrait. I look at young Betsy with the intensity with which I've gazed at older Betsy and I ask the same things: Tell me who you are. Tell me how to get to know you better.

Someone has written on the bottom of the photograph the words "A Family group." The occasion is the wedding on April 27, 1918 of my grandmother, Delia Lathrop Ross—Betsy—to my grandfather, Arthur Pier Root. The people in the photograph are, from right to left, Arthur, Betsy, Betsy's father, Charles W. G. Ross, her mother, Mary Lathrop Ross, Arthur's mother, Evalina Pier Donaldson Root, and his father, Winfield Scott Root. Perhaps Betsy's twin sister Helen or younger sister Jean took the picture, in the yard outside the Ross home in Cooperstown. It's the only photo I have of the event.

They had been high school sweethearts, children of well-established Cooperstown families; her Lathrop lineage there was three generations long, and their fathers were sometimes business partners. Art had graduated from Cooperstown High School in 1913, Betsy in 1914. The article about their wedding in *The Freeman's Journal* claimed that Delia was "one of Cooperstown's most charming and accomplished young ladies," known for playing piano and organ and singing in church. She and Art were regarded as being "among Cooperstown's most popular young people."

"SOLDIER WEDS," the headline reads; "Delia Lathrop Ross Becomes Bride of Arthur Pier Root." Title and subtitle seem to be wrestling with uncertainty about whom to emphasize in the news. "A simple wedding, hastened somewhat by conditions of war, was quietly solemnized at the home of Mr. and Mrs. Chas. W. G.

Ross," we're told. "There were no attendants and only the immediate members of the two families were present for the ceremony. The bride's gown was a becoming suit of blue serge with black hat and she wore a corsage of white roses." Arthur stands erect in uniform; the marriage has been expedited because, while a senior at Hamilton College, he was called into the armed forces, then chosen for Officers Training Camp at Camp Devens in Massachusetts, where he was recommended for a second lieutenant's commission, and is expected to be sent to France soon. Betsy is expected to graduate from Albany State Teacher's College in 1919, majoring in chemistry, but has volunteered with the Red Cross, hoping to be sent overseas but destined to serve nearer Cooperstown—it's against Red Cross policy to send a wife into a combat zone where her husband is serving. Shortly after this picture was taken the couple "left by trolley for a week's honeymoon trip in New York City."

Delia and her mother strike a similar pose, smiling at the camera. The bride's father—I remember seeing him in an earlier family photograph as a 13 year old boy leaning on his mother's shoulder; here he is a 62 year old man with little more than two years left to live—and the groom's mother are pleasantly cooperative for the photographer, but the figure everyone notices in this picture is the groom's father, the man who stands a little apart, somewhat shaded, with his arms folded across his chest, and a humorless glower on his face. The space between him and his wife is a noticeable gap.

The explanation for his pose usually given is that the fathers were business partners in Root & Ross, a tombstone business, more politely referred to as marble dealers. Because of either business problems or mere cussedness, W. S. disapproved of his son marrying C. W. G.'s daughter. The story is told by the couple's descendants that, earlier on the wedding day, Arthur found himself inexplicably locked in the bathroom. Certainly the picture suggests that something has irritated Arthur's father and that he has refused to join in the festive spirit of the day.

Part of what first captured my attention in this photo was the surprise of seeing my grandparents starting out together. Arthur is the only one of the group I remember, though Betsy lived until I was five years old and great-grandfather Root until I was eight. My other great-grandparents died before I was born, Charles Ross in 1920, Mary Ross in 1939, Evalina Root in 1940. I never knew Arthur very well, though I was in his presence many times before he died in 1961. But here my grandparents are, a century ago, different people from those I remember in separate formal portraits in my family's living room, the portraits I conjure whenever someone mentions them.

The other aspect of the photograph that captures my attention is the way it somehow parallels my parents' wedding. They too were married, in February 1942, with a World War in progress, and my father too would soon be going off to military service. There may have been friction between my parents' families as well, though I have no record of it on film or in anecdote, just the knowledge that the families were from different worlds to begin with, the vague sense that my mother was ill at ease around my father's family, the awareness that my mother's mother felt she and her husband were disapproved of by my father's family.

All this is my perception, my sense of things of course, and all this may apply to what came after, not the way people felt on their wedding day. Surely on this wedding day of Arthur and Betsy and on the wedding day of Bob and Marie twenty-four years later the bridal couples were happy to be getting what they most wanted.

Which is what you ought to feel on your wedding day.

I center my gaze on Betsy. I think I see here the charmed and charming young lady the newspaper mentions. There is a certain energy in her expression, in her stance, a suggestion that her father-in-law's grumpiness has no effect on her. And upright Arthur, at the opposite end of the row from his father, seems too pleased to be beside her to worry about his father.

Somehow I don't recognize Betsy in this photo as the woman in the 1947 Arizona portrait, the one taken close to the end of her life. It gives me pause. To what extent, I wonder, am I seeing the same woman in those two images? How do you measure the distance between the person someone appears to be in a photograph and the person she actually is in life?

All the family - Cooperstown 1926

In most of the photos I have of my father as a young child, he and his brother wear the identical outfit, as if they were twins. Arthur Pier Jr. was actually born in 1920, a year earlier than my father, Robert Lathrop, born in 1921. Their sister Frances, usually pictured between them, was born in 1923, the same year as my mother. I have only one photo of the entire family. In it my grandfather, Art Sr., seems cooperative but not entirely cheerful; my father, the little boy standing in front of him, seems more pensive than happy. Art Jr. has the brightest smile, Frannie a sweet sense of ease.

Alone of the group, my grandmother Betsy looks down while everyone else looks at the camera. I want to say her expression is demure, but I don't know if I'm reading it correctly. Her gaze doesn't really seem to be centered on the children. Oddly, it mirrors the disengaged gaze of the woman behind the three Ross girls in the earliest picture I have of my grandmother. On my computer I've enlarged it several times, in hopes of a more accurate reading of her expression, but remain uncertain what to make of it.

These pictures are family images borrowed from my cousin's collection. When I scanned her photos into my computer, I arranged them chronologically as best I could, trying to not only chart the growth of my father and his siblings but, in a sense, the westward movement of his family. My grandfather worked for the New York Telephone Company in Syracuse when Art and Rob were born; when Fran was born they lived in Auburn. Later they moved to East Aurora, in Erie County, and then to Buffalo, where Art Sr. had become a manager for the telephone company's division there. Eventually they settled twenty-five miles north, in Lockport, where the children would grow up and where my father would meet my mother. I have pictures of the three children when they were older, the boys no longer dressing alike, the girl always the one in the center of the picture.

The photos tell me more than what people I knew looked like before I was born. They tell me of family resemblances—often I see my father in my grandmother's face when she was younger; they tell me of persistent personality traits—as a boy my father seems more steadily confident and comfortable with himself, more assured and relaxed than his older brother; they tell me of persistent relationships—the siblings seem close knit, especially Fran and Rob, and suddenly memories from my own lifetime confirm this.

Or do my memories inspire the reading I give the photos, so that they conform to the perspective from which I hadn't realized I had always viewed them? Trying to know things for certain I seem to keep confirming how tentative all my knowledge is. Often my understanding is considerably less than certain. What is Betsy thinking in this photograph? Why isn't she looking at the camera?

The caption written in longhand across the bottom frame of the other family photograph I have tells me it was taken in Cooperstown in 1926, very likely in the yard around the Ross house at 2 Chestnut Street. I can't tell if it was taken the same year as the photo of the whole Root family or not. My grandmother and Frannie sit on the lawn, Frannie's smile wide and carefree. The boys are in matching costumes again, standing beside their grandmother's chair. Art Jr. has his hand on the arm of her chair; my father's arm is around her, his hand resting on her shoulder. He leans casually against the chair and coincidentally his pose echoes that of his grandfather Ross as a boy in a family photo from 1868. This is only the second picture in which my great-grandmother, Mary Lathrop Ross, appears, eight years older than in her daughter's wedding picture, a widow now after her husband's death six years earlier. Perhaps my grandfather, Art Root, or one of Betsy's sisters, Helen or Jean, took the picture. I don't know who inscribed the caption, but I've compared the handwriting to Betsy's and know she didn't write it.

It's not really a good photograph, the image a little blurry rather than sharp and clear, but even so, I notice a certain intensity in the gaze of both mother and grandmother. Art and Fran are cheerful, Rob pleasantly cooperative, but Mary has a tightness to her smile and Betsy barely attempts a smile. It's not an angry look, her eyes fixed on the camera and the photographer, but it's not a look that matches those of her children. Instead it matches the look of her mother, as if they've been roped into this family pose. Is the caption "All the family Cooperstown 1926" ironic or sardonic?

I flash back to the other family photograph, all the Roots together in a backyard, possibly even this one, but not on the same day. It's risky to make assumptions about family relationships based on a few random photographs. Shots taken minutes apart can evoke different reactions to the people depicted in them. Nonetheless I take the risk far enough to think that the two pictures don't capture the sense of family I interpret from anecdote and surviving texts, though if I recall the expression on Delia's face at the Glimmerglass, I feel I recognize her in this maternal role.

I'm cautious about making any kind of judgment based on these images. Elsewhere I have two photographs taken minutes apart of my mother with a little girl in First Communion dress who would only briefly, only temporarily, become her stepdaughter. In one photo my mother seems merry and vivacious and affectionate, and in the other she seems annoyed and dour and remote; in both the little girl seems guarded and on edge. Seems. If I didn't know that my mother's marriage to the little girl's father lasted less than a year, that the little girl and her older sister were unhappy the whole time

100

they lived with us—if we all had lived happily ever after—how differently would I read those images?

With my grandmother's image I have even less than a clear narrative to influence me. I have the evidence of her final portrait mounted on our living room wall for at least thirty years after her death as testimony to my father's love for her; I have my aunt's notes about the household she grew up in, the one that I suspect she modeled her own on, as separate testimony. Still, I can feel how distant I am from her when I stare at these images. How close can I get to her through photographs? How much closer have I actually gotten to anyone in life?

How to Develop
Your Personality

By Betsy Root

FASCINATING NEW WOMAN'S FEATURE—STARTS TOMORROW

offering daily advice on character building,
personal adjustment, vocational guidance, etc.

See the First Article in this New Series in Tomorrow's

COURIER-EXPRESS

How To
Develop Your
Personality

By BETSY ROOT

Did you ever stop to think that there is just one thing that makes you different from everyone else on earth? There is just one asset you have that no one can take from you and no one can ever duplicate—and that is your Personality—the outward expression of your character.

You may have unusual beauty, but your looks can never sum up You; your voice may be unusually lovely and appealing, but the sound of it can never fully express You. Only the wise development and use of Personality can reveal the You-ness of You.

Wouldn't you like to learn how to be successful? (I am not referring specifically to financial success, though that may well follow.) Surely you have often wished that you could make people really understand and appreciate you; you have longed to be a leader in the social, business and club activities that interest you most. The key to the situation is yours. Will you let us help you find and use it?

We are all familiar with the couplet from the pen of Bobbie Burns:
"Ah! wad some power the gittle gi'e us
To see ourselves as others see us!"

Every day this column, like a mirror held up before you, will show you your personality and its power.

The ad in the Sunday April 4, 1937 *Buffalo Courier-Express* announcing the column "How to Develop Your Personality" by Betsy Root called it a "FASCINATING NEW WOMAN'S FEATURE" that would be "offering daily advice on character building, personal adjustment, vocational guidance, etc." A photograph dominated the ad, Betsy's head slightly turned to fix her gaze on the reader, enough of her outfit exposed to suggest quietly stylish taste, her expression earnest and confident. She was 41 at the time. The column ran for nineteen weeks, six days a week for all but one of those weeks, 113 articles overall. We don't know how she came to write the column and we don't know why it ended, though it's likely that Betsy's health was a significant factor. In an era of handwritten drafts and typed copy delivered to the printer by hand or by daily mail, Betsy's travels for her health probably made keeping up a daily column difficult—though the column ran until August 14, as early as June 7 she promised to answer mail promptly because "it is possible that you may not read this column long. I am in need of rest and am going away for awhile." Or perhaps either she or the publisher came to feel that the feature had run its course.

One of the things we can wonder is what happened in the interval between the end of World War I, the Great War, when she was a Red Cross volunteer and her husband a second lieutenant in the army, and the beginning of the column eighteen years later. Yes, we know she had her children in 1920, 1921, and 1923, each born in Cooperstown though she and her husband lived in different New York cities in those years, and yes, we know that 2 Chestnut Street in Cooperstown was for her and her children a center of family reunion.

What did my grandmother do with her life in the ten years between that backyard photo and the start of her newspaper column? In that interval, the birth of her youngest child having triggered in her a dormant asthma, Betsy persistently needed to be somewhere other than western New York for a portion of the year. My wife also has asthma and, of late, we spend time in the fall away from the ragweed that heightens her allergies and confines her to indoor solitude. If we go to, say, Seattle, where she would be ragweed free, she walks the streets and spends hours outdoors daily, as she cannot do back home. Betsy sought that kind of relief herself, in a number of different environments.

One story in family lore has Betsy taking Art Jr., Rob, and Frannie to South Carolina, hoping the kids could go to school there while their mother evaded the stress of her western New York environment. Knowing little of South Carolina history, the boys were deemed to be behind a grade, and Rob was diagnosed as carrying tuberculosis and kept out of school. He was confined to the sun porch of their rental home, though Aunt Fran remembers that the quarantine didn't keep her and Art Jr. from playing games with him on his porch. He was later discovered to be free of tuberculosis. Back north, in Lockport, he skipped a grade and graduated early.

There were consequences to that.

But what I intimate from the little evidence I have is that Betsy tried to be a consistent mother to her children and that there were periods where mother and children were separated from father and husband, until eventually mother went alone to her physiological refuges and the children stayed home with their father, becoming teenagers, growing into young adults.

And toward the end of that ten-year period, Betsy became a columnist on the theme "How to Develop Your Personality." She seems not to have been formally educated in psychology. In her June 4 entry, to reinforce her assertion that "we must speak carefully if we would avoid harming anyone," she tells us:

The writer of this series sees, almost daily, both tragic and happy results of the power of the spoken word. Briefly to recall something of her experience, so that you may know how and why she sees these things: Her enlistment for service with the Red Cross service interrupted (as it happened, terminated) a college course which would have ended with a medical degree from Cornell Medical College. All the interests of life have centered around the use of applied psychology. For years she has worked as a character analyst . . . as hundreds of you know.

The series ran for only a few months and, according to the column itself, grew out of her tendency to consult and confer with people—she mentions consultations with individuals in families and lectures to different groups—because of her interest in and knowledge of the development of personality. She had intended to study chemistry at Albany State College and made her way partly through her talent playing piano and organ and singing in church, but nothing suggests a background in psychology. Nevertheless, the column evidences a great deal of reading in at least the popular texts of the field, and the columns suggest a certain level of familiarity with currents of thought about psychology in the 1930s.

For any of us in her family the crucial question is what the column tells us about Betsy as a person, as a mother, as a consultant to people who might have gained from her advice about developing personality. How does what she says about personality reflect on the ways her children—and in consequence her grandchildren and possibly her great-grandchildren—developed into the people they became?

*   *   *

The opening paragraphs of the first installment of "How to Develop Your Personality," published Monday, April 5, 1937, have a lively, conversational tone. They engage the reader personally in the first sentence—"Did you ever stop to think . . ."—addressing her directly, as if it were part of an intimate and genial interaction. The parallel structures of the first two sentences in the second paragraph balance one another and emphasize the reader's individuality: "You may have unusual beauty, but your looks can never sum up You;

104

your voice may be unusually lovely and appealing, but the sound of it can never fully express You." The third paragraph speculates on the kinds of success the reader may hope for, asserts that the "key to the situation is yours," and modestly offers to "help you find and use it." In the remainder of that day's column she asks the reader to play a game with her: she will explain the nature of personality and provide examples of the benefits of understanding it and the reader will try "honestly to analyze [herself] in the light of the suggestions made from day to day." The column assumes the tone and atmosphere of a pleasant but informed consultation with a friend.

I think the column is well worth the reading in its own right and, happily, my wife, who earned her doctorate in psychology some forty years after the column was written, appreciates its generosity and earnestness while noting the datedness of some of its academic ideas. But I've mostly read and reread it in hopes of having—or perhaps overhearing—a remote conversation with my grandmother.

By the time I tracked down, reproduced, and edited all the columns in the "How to Develop Your Personality" feature, I'd corresponded with my aunt and heard some family stories. Certain passages in the column caught my attention, passages meant to be anecdotal support for advice to column readers that resonated within my memory as elements of family history. Sometimes Betsy would be forthright about drawing on her own experience; other times I would discern or recognize or—yes—imagine that the unnamed characters she presented were veiled or anonymous portrayals of her children or herself.

One thread of the column centers on childrearing. Betsy mentions raising three children and sometimes the anecdotes and vignettes she offers in support of certain themes seem (to me) circumspectly to draw on the experiences of herself and her children. For example, she insists on the need to let a child find his or her own personality. That requires the parent to allow a certain latitude to the child's development—it's alright to insist on certain values but don't steer the child toward parent-chosen careers or life choices. She tells of children trying unhappily to carry out parental aspirations for them, as when the parents push them toward business careers while the children's instincts point them toward artistic ones. In one vignette someone's son starts hanging around with a shallow, negative boy, so the parents invite that boy and several more mature, more gracious boys to a party, with the result that the son chooses to pal around with the more positive role models. In another vignette a mother, observing her daughter's too insistent dependence on her, finds a way to be absent for days or weeks at a time. With the help of the father, the child learns independence and self-reliance—Betsy is a strong advocate of both.

She also offers a sympathetic reading of the angst of teenage boys in her May 1 column. She advises parents who feel they have lost "an intimate personal touch with their sons and daughters in the years of adolescence" to remember "their own sense of puzzled questioning in their own years of puberty," so that they can recognize how the child's awareness of "new adjustments that must come with his growth during this period" might be accompanied by "a temporary loss of stability." As she argues that physical changes in a child can provoke mental anxiety, making him wary of the "responsibilities of maturity" and distrustful of "his new sex-consciousness," the male pronoun may not simply be a convention of the era but may connect to her observation of her own teenaged sons. When she writes, "The new interest and curiosity about the opposite sex make him timid, afraid that perhaps he is thinking too much of these things," the comment strikes me as gleaned from experience. And in the very next paragraph, where she endorses the need for parents to use patience with children "during those years of adjustment, " she tells us she's reached that conclusion "as the result of personal experience in bringing up three children, and from observation, more or less intimate, of the work of other parents."

In the vignettes she relates to support her advice I suspect she's drawing on her life and her children's lives. The daughter with too much dependence on her mother might well be Fran, the mother who travels in order to help the child become more independent must be Betsy herself, the father who offers cooperation and understanding in the scheme to help the daughter must be my grandfather. And the teen-age boys wrestling with the onset of sexual maturity and near adulthood must be my father and his brother.

Betsy's daughter has referred to her parents' child-rearing philosophy as a "kind of benign neglect. [. . .] They tried to teach by example, respect the child, support him always, but let him make his own mistakes." In her April 16 column, Betsy advises:

> Let your child grow in the most natural way. Guide and control him as seems best; but don't get in his way. Love can be just as much a hurdle to a child as selfishness. Try to give your youngster good sense, good taste, a definite religious concept (Faith), a sense of moral values . . . all the things he will need to mold his character. But let his personality flower of itself.

In regard to child-rearing at least, what Betsy advocated in her column was something that she'd already put into practice in her children's lives.

*   *   *

I suspect that anyone who writes an advice column like "How to Develop Your Personality" has to draw often, as surreptitiously as possible, on the columnist's life experiences. Even when the columnist's intentions are meant to reinforce broader recommendations about behavior, singling out family members or friends for critical analysis in public media can easily be read as imprudent gossip unless a certain amount of tact and subterfuge is taken. Nonetheless, the columnist's inner circle may be able to guess from where specific references are drawn.

As Betsy's curious and probing grandson, and with varying degrees of confidence, I trust my intuitions when I attempt to identify the real-life sources of the examples she shares, particularly when I stumble on parallels in her own life. For example, references in her column of Wednesday, April 21, 1937, make me certain I know whom she's writing about.

It opens: "Beware of the 'missionary of personality' . . . the person who wants everyone to have a personality exactly like his, or her, own." Ostensibly it's a column arguing against the impulse to make others conform to a behavior different from their already established character. She tells us of "a young woman staying in my home in whose future I was very much interested," who, despite a certain amount of charm and talent, "suffer[ed] a good deal [. . .] just because she tried to make someone over." The woman, who was being courted by a friend of Betsy and her husband, became insistent that her suitor should alter his tastes and his style; eventually she alienated him to the point that he avoided not only her but also his friends. "Long before the girl left us to move to another city, we had lost all chance of visiting with the young man," Betsy tells us. She then advocates strongly for the idea that "each man and woman has sifted for his use certain attributes which go to make up his particular individuality" and argues against others interfering with it. As a sidenote, she also mentions that "three years later that young woman enlisted in the missionary service of her church and has for some years been doing marvelous work in the Far East." It's almost a happy ending for the young woman, redirecting her inclinations in a more promising direction for herself.

As serviceable as the example is for the theme of the column, hints in the piece point to a specific source for the story: the introductory metaphor "missionary of personality," the "young woman staying in my home," her having "enlisted in [. . .] missionary service" and "doing marvelous work in the Far East." This surely is a column about Arthur Root's older sister Florence. My intuition is reinforced by passages in Ronald B. Detrick's biography of Florence Root, *Great Is Thy Faithfulness,* which claim her youthful aimlessness "landed her in Syracuse, where she lived with her younger brother Arthur and his wife" and that later, as a missionary in Korea, her personality "included a non-nonsense, direct approach to things, even in prayer." It's difficult to believe that Florence is not the young woman in Betsy's column.

Detrick's biography draws heavily on Florence's own writing, including an autobiographical sketch she wrote in 1974, a host of personal correspondence, and annual Missionary Correspondence Letters. I learn from it that Florence, who first served in Korea in 1927, was first on leave back to the United States in 1932 and in 1938 "made her furlough home in Lockport, New York, with her brother Arthur and his family," according to a "personal communication" from my aunt, Fran. (Detrick never names Arthur's wife.) Betsy and Florence interacted occasionally during her retreat from wartime Korea from 1942 to 1945—she played the organ at Betsy's daughter's wedding "to an airman" in 1943—and I likely met her as a toddler at some time then. Detrick quotes a passage from a letter Florence wrote in 1952, when she was again back in the U S to avoid the havoc of the Korean War, in which she tells of spending a week "in Lockport, near Buffalo, with my brother Arthur and two of his married children and their lovely children, six in all"—my sister, my brother and I would have been three of the children, Aunt Fran's first two daughters and first son were the other three. I surely met her then, when I was ten years old. My vague memory of an older woman in my grandfather's house may well have been of Grandaunt Florence on that visit, when she was nearly sixty and Betsy had been dead for five years. Florence died in 1995, at the age of nearly 102, in a Presbyterian retirement home in Virginia.

I scanned Florence's biography thoroughly in hopes of confirming Betsy's column more solidly but it is overwhelmingly about her missionary work from 1927 to 1978. Early in the book Detrick quotes from her autobiographical sketch about how she chose to break her engagement to "a most desirable 'catch'" because her "desire to marry decreased." Her brother Charles told the biographer that Florence's mother Eva Root had talked her out of it. Detrick speaks of her having "turned her back on marriage" and looking for something more meaningful in her life beyond teaching, eventually finding the missionary calling. Betsy's story might be about a different, later relationship that never developed into a prospective marriage, but it may well be about the engagement Florence herself alludes to, adapted to suit the tenor of the column.

And all at once I find myself in Betsy's position, writing about family members in less veiled commentary than she did, and suddenly aware that their versions of these events might read quite differently. I'm only on the far edges of Betsy's inner circle, accessing only her literary remains, what she's gone public with, and contending with the possibility of contradiction by considering Florence's literary remains. Did Florence ever read that column about the "missionary of personality" who went on to do "marvelous work in the far east"? If so, did she feel fairly (if anonymously) represented? Did she recall her mother talking her out of a potential marriage (as her brother claims she did) or having her "desire to marry decreased" on her own (as she claimed in her autobiography)? Did Betsy later have any misgivings about presenting her sister-in-law (anonymously) as an example of such a problematic personality? If I had known Aunt Florence but never read her biography, would I have read Betsy's column differently?

Asking unanswerable questions seems to be a habit with me now. But considering this column of Betsy's in the light I have, I can't help wondering whether she would think I represented it fairly. Or if she would think, perhaps uncomfortably, that I was earnestly trying to carry on a model she set for me long before I knew it existed.

*　　　*　　　*

When writing a daily column, one day's entry can influence the next day's entry. Betsy's column often adapts a thematic approach week by week, letting her introduce a concept and then accumulate a short series amplifying her thinking about it. When we're composing, we open synapses that lead not only to related bits of knowledge but also to related bits of memory. Occasionally, reading "How to Develop Your Personality" in sequence, I sense a relationship among vignettes that seem as much personal as thematic, giving me some insight into a recurring thread connecting expressions of her own development and personality.

For example, that mention in the May 1 column encouraging parents dealing with the confusion of their teenage children to remember their own "puzzled questioning" in puberty perhaps prompts a more elaborate vignette of development in the May 3 column. Asserting that experience is the best developer of personality, she tells us,

> I've known intimately for many years a woman who learned through experience, and who knows now, as she looks back over life, that all experience both good and bad is a gift. Everything that happens to her she considers as a challenge, as though Fate said to her, "Here is something new to face. Are you strong enough to get some good out of it . . . or will it beat you?"

She claims that when the woman was "about eighteen years old, living in circumstances of financial ease, abundant health, and social popularity," she expressed contempt and insensitivity about the sick and the poor of the world, considering them stumbling blocks to progress, an attitude "smug, complacent and ignorant of life."

> What happened to her? Fate took the silly little strand of her life and wove it into the intimate tapestry of her own

110

little family. She loved and married a poor man and knew at times real poverty; she bore three children who were so dear to her that their problems taught her patience and wisdom. She suffered long illness after the children were born and had to learn the meaning of pain. And all this made a woman of her.

Because her lot fell in with a man who needed her help, because her love for him and their children was so deep, because life taught her the patience of pain, all the joys of living have been increased, too. All her happiness has been intensified because she can compare it to difficult things. Love and joy are the high lights that stand out in bold relief against the shadows of sorrow and struggle.

This capsule account of the woman's life confirms Betsy's assertion that hard experience can change someone's personality for the better.

But the column also stirs echoes in me in the way the story of the woman she has "known intimately" recapitulates aspects of Betsy's own life. The parallels with Betsy's life—the security of her childhood and adolescence, the marriage and bearing of three children, the onset of illness and pain—are strong. Betsy's circumstances at eighteen, around 1913, were certainly secure and affluent: she grew up in the house of her grandfather, Horace Lathrop, referred to in an obituary as "the Beloved Physician," with her parents and sisters; her great-grandfather, also Horace Lathrop, had been a prominent lawyer; her father, Charles Ross, was a successful businessman. In other columns she alludes to the trials of her situation on her personality. On April 24, she tells us, "I was once definitely threatened with the spiritual stagnation and cessation of character development that accompanies idleness as [the idle affluent] are." On June 2, she admits, "All my life I needed so much guidance and strength, needed to conquer temper, to stimulate ideals and avoid complacence and smugness." These characterizations of her own struggles remind me of that young woman "so smug, complacent, and ignorant of life."

I'm not sure how much her comments about the woman's circumstances in marriage and mothering exaggerate the circumstances of her own marriage and mothering. Art Root certainly was, if not outright poor, a man who had to provide for them all. His work with the New York Telephone Company led them to move five times in thirteen years. During the Depression, the family endured considerable financial hardship, exacerbated by Betsy's illness and her need to find more hospitable climates for a portion of each year. Her daughter remembers their having to sell the grand piano that the family gathered around while Betsy played and both parents sang. She also recalls her father paying off medical debts from the town they lived in when she began elementary school some fifteen years after they'd moved and after her own daughter was born. Years after Betsy's death, my father met my grandfather in the Tuscarora Club in Lockport to celebrate Art's finally paying off the last of Betsy's medical bills. In that April 24 column, directed at the idle affluent, she says wryly, "I've been definitely promoted to the ranks of the poor, who have plenty to do."

For the woman in the vignette, all these trials resulted in "all the joys of living being increased." The cheerful earnestness and positive thinking of the column are echoed in the description of the woman's outlook on life, an outlook that Betsy describes with an intimacy that avoids mention of how she knows about this outlook. It may well be that Betsy's continual interaction with other people has nourished in her this powerful sense of empathy that underlies so many of the columns in the series. I can't prove otherwise. But my instincts suggest that there's a certain element of self-therapy running through the column, a kind of ghost memoir that, rather than stand back from it as such a column might let me do, invites me to intuit my grandmother's personality, draw closer to it, and feel as if I'm getting to know her.

An artifact associated with my grandmother Betsy Root: a note in her own hand. On June 26th, 1941, Betsy Root wrote this to Marie Linderman, to accompany a graduation gift of hand-decorated linen. I chanced upon it browsing through one of my mother's albums long after her death and long after my father's death. I was surprised to find it and even more surprised by how moved I was to hear my grandmother's voice on the page.

And what is the voice I hear? It was a different world seventy years ago. Perhaps my mother, who had had a hope chest, pasted newspaper clippings about weddings into her scrapbook, and thought about marriage a great deal, wouldn't have been surprised to receive the gift of a luncheon set and would have been encouraged by the effort her boyfriend's mother put into its creation. But it's my grandmother who is revealed on the page—the liveliness of her expression, pleasant, polite, charming and self-deprecating, affectionate if not entirely familiar.

The gift comes shortly after Marie's commencement and eight months before my parents' marriage. I don't know if the wedding was already being planned—they married two months after Pearl Harbor and America's entry into World War Two—but Betsy must have expected Rob to marry Marie and felt a need to establish a rapport with her. Rob would have been the first of her children to marry and perhaps Betsy hoped to have a compatible relationship with her daughter-in-law. She alludes to "our Buffalo spree" as if it had been proposed in the past. In knitting the luncheon set she was preparing to surrender to my mother a portion of a family heirloom, the linen "spun and woven by Rob's great-great-great grandmother" anywhere from 100 to 150 years earlier. The ancestor likely was Sarah Budger Lathrop (1753-1847), who died in her 94th year and reached the midpoint of her life at the turn of the 19th century. It wasn't the kind of object to give up casually and Betsy's efforts in her illness and graciousness in the note suggest an attempt to bond somehow with my mother.

If I seem to give the note too much significance, it's because, before I found it, I have never had any sense of Betsy Root's relationship with my mother. My father spent my earliest years away in the Marines, serving in the Pacific, and I have no memory of having been with her, ever having seen her, ever having heard her voice—surely I had—in the short time between my birth and her death. I had no way to know what Grandma Root had been like. In my mother's family, at random times, I sometimes had dour hints of the aloofness, of the superiority, her family thought the Roots had exhibited. It was suggested that my father's parents had disapproved of Rob's marriage, that they thought *their* son too good for the daughter in a working class family. Living in the thick of my mother's side of my family, I intuited a class difference on my father's side and never quite felt myself a part of my father's family.

I don't know how my mother responded to my grandmother's gift. She may have welcomed an heirloom addition to her trousseau; she may have felt a twinge of discomfort at the values of her boyfriend's mother, a defensive awareness that his background and hers were not aligned. Being uncomfortable about more educated and accomplished people is not actually evidence of their disdain; it may be more evidence of our insecurity. Whose self-consciousness, my mother's or her mother's, was at play in this attitude? How much of it was reliably based on Betsy's behavior? Whether she had misgivings or not is more difficult to prove, though, in retrospect, it would not be difficult to justify.

Here are two things I know: The note to accompany the luncheon set testifies that Betsy was gracious enough to make some sort of effort to be welcoming; my mother's keeping the note until the end of her life suggests that she never took it to be an insignificant message.

*   *   *

And there is something else I've since learned. During the war, when my aunt, my father's sister, was considering marriage to an Air Force cadet, her mother sent her letters of support, knowing that her daughter's situation was one she had lived with herself. "I shall be living all these months very close to you in thought," she wrote, "for you are repeating my own history so intimately. . . . you may come to feel that you want to be his before he goes away. I should understand that for it was a great comfort to me when Dad was in France to feel that I was his, proudly and irrecoverably." When I read these lines I remember the wedding photo from 1918, Art in uniform, Betsy demurely by his side, their faces lit by a sense of joyful fulfillment.

The letter is loving and affectionate but in its intimacy I also hear the voice of the columnist, confirming my sense of how naturally she wrote. She balances her support for marriage before my aunt's beloved is sent overseas with consideration of the alternative of waiting until his return. "But if you choose the hard way, and decide to wait, I'll try to help you during your waiting. If one loves enough, even waiting is supremely worth it. Don't emphasize, even in your own mind, sweetheart, your youth. You at twenty are so much wiser, so much more grown up, so much more sophisticated than I was at twenty-two." The endearments punctuating the letter only confirm that Betsy was someone who practiced what she preached.

When my aunt, then stationed in San Diego, confirmed the decision to marry in a "special delivery air mail letter," the immediate reply from her parents was a telegram that read, "Approval axiomatic!" Betsy's individual reply, composed, as she said, "just about 40 minutes" after the air mail letter arrived, reveals the depth of her feelings about having shared in her daughter's decision. She confirms that the telegram "goes out with our 'God bless you', darling, from hearts full of only wishes for your happiness," and then confesses, "I shall never be able to tell you adequately in words how much it made me feel our close kinship, that you should write me 'woman to woman' as you did, sweetheart." No wonder my aunt treasures these letters and that telegram. No wonder her granddaughter, Betsy's great-granddaughter, drew on them for a show she devised and choreographed about the war.

Each time I read Betsy's note to my mother and interchange with my aunt I am convinced of her sincerity and her compassion. Each reading brings her substantially more alive to me.

"The house was very large and very, very quiet."

So Betsy's novel begins. It's a terse and evocative opening sentence, and in the paragraph that follows she expands on the mood it creates:

> "It made me feel all queer inside to think of how many people were in the house and yet how still it was. Everyone was waiting. Not only the people, but even the silent house itself . . . except for the old banjo clock in the hall, whose staid ticking ignored the silence . . . seemed waiting. All waiting for Grandfather to die."

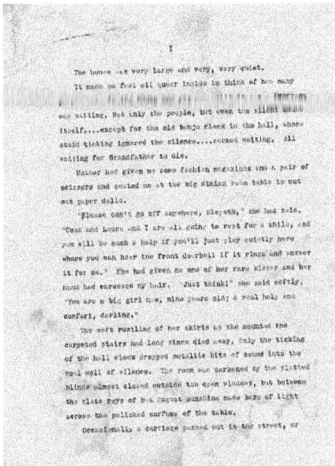

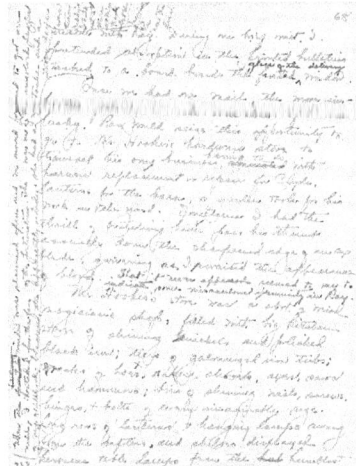

Except for her mention of feeling queer about the silence, the narrator only gives us subtle clues about her emotions in the opening scene. Assigned to sit at the dining room table cutting paper dolls out of fashion magazines while the grown-ups rest, she only hints at some remoteness between herself and her mother ("She had given me one of her rare kisses and her hand had caressed my hair") and concentrates on inhabiting the scene and creating an air of expectancy.

> The soft rustling of her skirts as she mounted the carpeted stairs had long since died away. Only the ticking of

the hall clock dropped metallic bits of sound into the cool well of silence. The room was darkened by the slotted blinds almost closed outside the open windows, but between the slats rays of hot August sunshine made bars of light across the polished surface of the table.

Occasionally a carriage passed out in the street, or someone walked past on the sidewalk. Each time, I paused in turning the leaves of the fashion books, and listened, half expecting footsteps to crunch upon the gravel path that led to our front door. But no one turned in, and the time dragged on.

I'm impressed by these opening pages. I immediately trust this narrator's voice. I want to see this world through her nine-year-old eyes and learn what Grandfather's death will mean for this child and for her family. It seems like a promising start for this novel.

Betsy began the novel in 1946, at the Tucson Medical Center ("Formerly the Desert Sanitorium") in Arizona. She wrote the opening pages on the backs of copies of a letter announcing a monthly Medical Staff meeting and page 11 of their by-laws, written in blue ink with a fountain pen. The sixty handwritten manuscript pages I have are numbered 55 through 114; the first 54 pages no longer exist, probably discarded after she typed them up on onion-skin paper. There are thirty-four typed pages in the existing manuscript. Prior to starting the novel, she had written and published short stories and attempted an autobiography; I haven't located any of the stories—no one in the family knows where she published them—and she destroyed the manuscript of the autobiography. The only published writing where I've heard her voice on the page is her psychology column, written nine years before the unfinished novel. The novel is an intriguing project, seeming to be a *roman à clef*, a fiction drawn specifically from the author's life with changes in identities, events, and circumstances disguising the real-life originals.

I'm certain that Elspeth, the narrator, is Betsy, though the parallels between them and their families are not exact. Elspeth is growing up in a house where she lives with her grandfather and her parents, apparently as an only child, a brother having been stillborn; Betsy grew up in her grandfather's house and lived there with her parents and two sisters, one of them her twin, the other younger, an older brother (Horace Lathrop Ross) and a younger sister both having died in infancy. Elspeth's father and grandfather are both doctors; Betsy's grandfather was a doctor but her father was a businessman. Like Elspeth's grandfather, Betsy's grandfather died in the house where they lived, when, like Elspeth, she was nine. The middle-class surroundings—large house, social position, servants—are as true of Betsy as of Elspeth. Elspeth's grandfather is not named, but her mother Mary's alcoholic brother is named Horace; Betsy's grandfather and great-grandfather were both named Horace and her mother's name was Mary, though she was called Minnie. In the novel Elspeth's Uncle Horace kills himself; in life Betsy's grandfather had two daughters and a son but at his death he was survived only by the daughters—I've been unable to learn what became of the son. Elspeth's father's family, the MacGregors, are Scots in origin; Betsy's father's family, the Rosses, originated in Scotland but emigrated from Ireland. There are parallels between Elspeth's parents and Betsy's: their mothers were born and raised in that small village, the daughters of doctors; their husbands were from away, Charles Wilbur Guyon Ross well traveled before arriving in Cooperstown.

A good deal of this could be the kind of drawing on life that most first-time novelists need to do. Writing about the world you know is commonplace, as first novels by established authors so frequently remind us. It's not that hard to notice the parallels if you know something about the author's life. More difficult to determine is the extent to which the relationships among the characters replicate the relationships among the people on which they're based. In Chapter V, long after Elspeth as narrator has slipped away from the child's perspective and assumed the voice of someone in her "present grandmotherly estate" (in 1946 Betsy's grandchildren included my cousin, my sister, and me), she tells us, "Whatever character I have, whatever vision concerning the character of others, and all my unswerving faith in God and His goodness had their genesis in that fire-lit study. Everything I ever learned elsewhere but supplements what my father taught me during those long and intimate hours." This declaration is spoken by Elspeth, but the focus on character and the affirmation of faith both echo moments in the advice column Betsy wrote ten years before she began the novel.

119

I'm certain that the attribution here is as much autobiography as it is fiction.

The first two chapters of my grandmother's manuscript are set in the family house leading up to and following from the death of Elspeth's grandfather. Nothing more is mentioned about Uncle Horace's suicide and midway through the second chapter Elspeth begins to leap ahead in time, to suggest that she is not the nine-year-old girl anymore but an adult looking back on childhood events. The chapters that follow the funeral in the second chapter become increasingly reminiscent and focused more on daily life, and even the third chapter, where Elspeth accompanies her mother and Miss Neilsen to the seashore "for a month's change and rest" after the trial of Grandfather's death, has little to say about either of the deaths in the first two chapters. Subsequent chapters read almost like something out of *Anne of Green Gables* or *Little House on the Prairie* or *Little Women,* accounts of routine events that bring the activities of Elspeth's little town to life.

In Chapter VII, one of the longer chapters, Elspeth accompanies Ray, her parents' coachman and handyman, in a trap behind the old horse Clyde, on a round of errands to several local businesses. She's at pains to record the conversations she overhears and details of the settings in "the market, the grocery, the Post Office, and sundry other places." She captures Ray's homespun dialect in his remarks to her and conversations with different grocers or the woman at the dairy store. Her descriptions of the people are individualized and pointed: "Mr. Barrett was charming, so genial and ingratiating always. He waited on his clientele in a spotless white coat, as distantly removed from Mr. Johnson's shabby blood-stained garments of similar cut and material as a Prince Albert is from a workman's blouse." "[Mr. Whipple] would lumber about, climbing up to high shelves, leaning down to low ones, opening and shutting bins and drawers, puffing and blowing as he worked. Every time he caught his breath, he'd whistle softly. Darling Nelly Gray seemed the only tune he knew; at least I never heard him whistle any other." "Mr. Hooker, a little man with a soft voice, a mane of snow white hair, and an immaculate person, presided like a high priest over his temple of trade. He waited on his customers, many of whom were shabby farm folk, with unfailing courtesy, clad always in an old black velvet jacket over a white shirt, and wearing a black, soft bow tie of generous proportions. He looked more like a poet than a hardware merchant." "[Mrs. Burris] was always dressed in a stiffly starched print dress, with a big white apron tied around her waist. The bib of the apron was anchored to her ample bosom with two small pins of hand-painted china that bobbed up and down in the most fascinating way when she walked." Each character is distinctive and described so fully that they seem entirely characters of their era, as well as people the author may well have viewed in life.

I have most of that chapter in Betsy's handwritten manuscript, and I notice the changes she makes as she composes, sometimes minor but sometimes significant in terms of bringing the scene to life. One insertion in the post office scene suggests the level of attention and perhaps recall that Betsy drew on. Elspeth's account of her visit to the post office originally ended with mention of Elspeth's activity there: "During our brief wait, I pretended absorption in the printed bulletins tacked to a board beside the frosted glass of the delivery window." But soon after she adds another one of her portraits of local characters.

> When the window was slammed open and we moved forward to get our mail, I watched for the face of the postmistress. She was one of the unsolved puzzles of my childhood, because, though apparently a lady, she had a mustache and a voice deeper even than Daddy's. I tried not to stare at Miss Beal but she fascinated me nonetheless.

I sense the child's fascination not simply because she declares it but also within the description itself.

I feel a similar sense of immediacy in her description of Ray's working on garden tools at the hardware store: "Sometimes, I had the thrill of watching him pass his thumb casually down the sharpened edge of an ax blade, quivering as I awaited the appearance of blood. That it never appeared seemed to me to indicate some miraculous immunity in Ray." I believe that's what Elspeth witnessed, which makes me feel as if that was also something Betsy witnessed.

*   *   *

As I read the manuscript I keep sensing its affinity with the column. For example, the eighth chapter offers an account of Elspeth's friendship with a rather solitary unmarried woman, Susan Hewitt, for whom her mother seems to have some antipathy. Near the end of the chapter Elspeth's father reassures Elspeth about Susan, who was his patient before his marriage to Mary. Susan's solitary life makes people wonder about her, but her father calls her "a very fine woman." He advises Elspeth to talk with Susan about questions that will arise as she grows up rather than bring them up with her reticent mother. Susan is an intriguing and well-developed character and their friendship is referred to in other parts of the manuscript. I wonder if the mention in the June 18 column of a "tiny woman who lives not far from Buffalo, whose faith and courage and high ideals have done more to help me than all the other influences in my life combined" isn't a reference to the real-life Susan Hewitt. Betsy says that, when she's "feeling 'low'" the woman helps her to "see again how trivial some things are, how much there is to laugh about in some of the things that have seemed important. She gives me back my sense of values."

The final chapters find Elspeth in a public high school rather than in boarding school or a more elite school her mother prefers. There she meets and befriends a wide range of young people, which troubles her mother. Elspeth wishes her mother could "have adapted herself as happily to my democratization as Daddy and I did." She tells us, "During my High School years, Mother became less and less accessible to me." Her mother's "attitude of increasing indifference might have wrought real havoc" in regard to "my physical development . . . and the psychological factors involved in a precocious puberty" if not for her father's having performed "many of the duties one would have presumed to be hers." She claims, "It was during that emotional transition that Susan Hewitt who 'had lots of common sense and practically no nerves'" [to quote her father] "gave of her patient sympathy and understanding as wisely as any mother could have done." While Mary "shudderingly dismissed me again and again," asserting that "ladies simply do not discuss such things," Elspeth asserts that "Susan's matter-of-fact treatment of my questionings about my changing self undoubtedly saved me from becoming a terror-ridden neurotic." She credits "Daddy's sound biological instruction, coupled with Susan's matter-of-fact treatment of my self-questionings," with giving her "a pretty stable adjustment." Of her mother she surmises: "If she doesn't understand all I'm feeling, all I'm seeking to learn, after having been married to Daddy and having his children, it must be because she never found anyone to talk intimately with her when she was my age. What fear and shock she must have endured, to experience marriage and childbirth, such lovely, desirable things, without understanding."

Elspeth declares that she "liked boys" and their attentions and was warned by her mother and friends about being taken advantage of. She writes,

> A few times in those gay and busy years, sex reared its head, but I didn't recognize it as ugly. To be truthful, I still don't. Sex is frequently, to the young, extremely clumsy and embarrassing in its timing. It is very probable that, confronted with fear and ignorance, it may become ugly. So far as my personal experience is concerned, I wouldn't know. I still believe sex is one of God's better gifts; and I'm glad to say my children feel the same way.

And here I find myself thrown back into her advice column.

It isn't only that in this chapter I hear no difference between the voice of the fictional narrator and the voice of the advice columnist in "How to Develop Your Personality" explaining what people think and feel. It's also that I hear echoes of her advice to parents about remembering "their own sense of puzzled questioning in their own years of puberty," in order to help their children deal with "a temporary loss of stability" in "those years of adjustment." That was the point where she claimed to learned this lesson "as the result of personal experience in bringing up three children, and from observation, more or less intimate, of the work of other parents."

*   *   *

And that's what the novel brings me back around to—the sense of Delia as a child, as a young woman. I can't know for certain what her relationship with her mother was like, can't know if it was her father she felt so close to. There are uncertainties in roman à clef, possibilities that figures out of autobiography have been assigned somewhat different fictional roles. Is Elspeth's father a doctor and not a businessman like Betsy's because Betsy's grandfather was the doctor that she felt close to? Is Betsy putting Elspeth in Minnie Ross's role, as a sympathetic interpretation of her own mother's life that someone writing first person fiction and having grown up in the same house and in the same village that her mother did cannot avoid coloring with an overlay of her own emotions and attitudes and memories?

I don't know. I can't know. I will never know. And so I am left with intuition, with imagination steeped in empathy and, frankly, longing. The Betsy of the psychology column could so easily be the child who once was Elspeth; the grandmother rendering the instances of Elspeth's life as if they were her own could easily be the earnest and attentive and compassionate advisor of the newspaper feature. I see Elspeth in the images of young Betsy, see young Betsy in the memories Mrs. Root shares in the column, hear her in the observant attention she gives to characters both remembered and imagined.

7

Dear Buddy,

I know you haven't used that name for
decades but thank you for using it now.
Buddy was my first grandchild, the earliest
of the three I actually got to meet. Thank
you for editing the newspaper column. I'm
sure your Aunt Fran and her children,
your cousins, were pleased and I
know your father and your uncle Art
would have been as well. Remember how
often I wrote about children becoming
themselves, finding their own paths to follow
and resisting the efforts of parents to
push them onto paths where they don't
feel comfortable. I think your life is
proof that my theory has merit — you
chose a path that no one expected but
was rooted (not only a pun) in who
you were. For all the distance between
us in life and all the distance over
the years following my death, your path
led you back around to getting to know
me at last. That was very nice of you.
I'm grateful.

Love,
Grandma Betsy

There is one thread in Betsy's column that I can't seem to avoid connecting with more fiercely than with the others. Part of her insistence on letting the child find his or her own way in the world grows out of her theory of inherited traits. In her April 16th column she claims, "Your child carries with him traits and characteristics descended to him from many generations of ancestors, not only those from his parents and grandparents. His origins are more deeply rooted, more powerfully endowed, than you and I can see. There may emerge in him talents and powers long buried in the past." She then introduces the idea of throwback traits, suggesting that interests and attitudes and talents displayed by someone in a family's past but suppressed in generations of descendants might arise again insistently, intensely in another family member. In the April 22 column she explains that "throw-backs" "are people who seem to

125

have attributes, talents, characteristics not apparent in their parents or grandparents. They derive from some obscure ancestor whose particular abilities seem to have lain dormant for some generations." Her supporting vignette concerns a young man from a Southern family with a "history and background closely affiliated with the administrative and business leadership of the state" who has a "God-given voice . . . one of the greatest possible promise" and becomes a successful operatic baritone. She also mentions another who is "a remarkable composer, though there have been no musicians in his family for many generations." Part of her discussion supports her belief that children should choose their interests, that "the effort to force a child to lead a career of family tradition might frequently lead to failure and disappointment . . . We don't do anything well unless our hearts are in it."

I'm not sure whether my own life confirms Betsy's throwback theory, but I'm attracted to it because, so far as I knew, I came from a long line of businessmen and laborers, my father a salesman, his father an executive, my mother's father and my uncles all factory workers, my mother a cashier and then a bank teller. When I went to college, I thought I was the first in either family to do that. Long after I graduated and followed my inclinations to became a teacher and a writer, I learned that my father's parents had gone to college and both of their family trees included college grads—clergymen, lawyers, doctors, teachers. It was only after I had married an asthmatic educator with a degree in psychology that I learned my grandmother had been an asthmatic writer of a psychology column, as well as a writer of stories and an unfinished novel. She had also been a musician, as my wife is. Some of those parallels clearly cannot be explained by Betsy's throwback theory— they are more fortunate coincidences, I suppose—but the desire for creative expression in me seems to be more than simply accidental given my grandmother's desire for the same thing. I somehow am sure that my struggles with the creative life might not have been so fierce and stumbling had my grandmother known me as I was growing up and recognized the intensity of my interest.

Something has accumulated here in text and image. If I can accept the unverifiable as certainty, impressions as sufficient evidence, hunches as equivalent to documentation, then I can feel as if I've come to know my grandmother. Betsy, in the spirit of judicious counseling, might advise me that feeling is not the same as knowing. I, in my insistent pragmatism, might answer that, at this late date in our tenuous relationship, perhaps feeling is sufficient enough.

Once, a few years ago, at a retreat at the Christine Center in western Wisconsin, our session leader assigned us to write a letter that couldn't be delivered, perhaps to a single person, real, imaginary, dead, living, in the past, in the future. I chose to write to Betsy.

"Grandma Root," I addressed her, "I'm sorry I don't remember you." I reminded her that I was five when she died and that, in my early childhood, she was often away for her health and my father was in the Pacific and my mother didn't work hard to keep me in touch with her. Then I explained that I had "edited your newspaper column and published it, not just to give to all your descendants—you have great-great-great grandchildren now—but because by reading you over and over again I hoped somehow to get to know you." I told her I thought I had somewhat, and that perhaps "I learned where my father's values came from and, through him, many of my own." In the end I wrote, "I think if I had had you in my life, my life would have been much different. I don't regret how it turned out, but I'd like to know who I would have become if you had known me." I signed it, "Love, Buddy," in hopes she would remember my childhood nickname.

Then the session leader asked us to write a letter in reply to ourselves from the person to whom we'd written. This is what "Betsy" wrote back to me.

Dear Buddy,

I know you haven't used that name for decades but thank you for using it now. Buddy was my first grandchild, the earliest of the three I actually got to meet. Thank you for editing the newspaper column. I'm sure your Aunt Fran and her children, your cousins, were pleased and I know your father and your Uncle Art would have been as well. Remember how often I wrote about children becoming themselves, finding their own paths to follow and resisting the efforts of parents to push them onto paths where they don't feel comfortable. I think your life is proof that my theory has merit—you chose a path that no one expected but was rooted (not only a pun) in who you were. For all the distance between us in life and all the distance over the years following my death, your path led you back around to getting to know me at last. That was very nice of you. I'm grateful.

Love,
Grandma Betsy

I notice that neither one of us refer to me as a "throwback," though some part of me believes that, if there's any merit to her theory, I should be considered an example of one—the writer kid who didn't know he had a writer grandmother until long after he'd committed to what seemed a quirky and idiosyncratic path.

I wonder about the honesty of what I wrote to her, how much more I might have said; I wonder about the possible sincerity of what I hoped she'd write back to me, not simply the effort to impersonate her voice but also the effort to capture what she might have felt had she been able to write the letter herself. After all, in that assignment we both were buoyed by optimism, the expectation—or at least the hope—that had we ever had a life together, this would have been how we would have felt, what we would have believed about each other.

Maybe that's the advantage of early loss. You get to choose the color of hope—you have to choose it. Betsy's Presbyterian faith was strong—she's open in the column about her beliefs and the need she feels for everyone to have some kind of faith; it's the faith my father practiced, the one my wife practices. I have no particular religion but I sometimes practice a vaguely Buddhist form of meditation, engaging in approaches that ask me to feel loving kindness, compassion, appreciative joy, or equanimity. I simply try to feel those qualities, to hover in those feelings as if they are being transmitted through some involuntary spiritual ether. If there were a way for what I feel to reach my grandmother somehow—a way I don't believe exists—I'm sure my feelings would reach her.

And so, as much as I've been claiming to write this as a way to come to know Betsy, perhaps I've also been writing this as a way for her to come to know me. This is as close to being in touch with one another as we'll ever be. All I can do now is feel what I feel and believe it's enough to be able to feel it.

Interlude: Locks

I open the album, really a set of blank three-ring notebook pages in a simple gray binder. I made several such albums that year, trying to organize my piles of photos into thematic units. This one is devoted to my hometown, Lockport, New York, grouping images into sections titled, somewhat pretentiously —"The Heart" (the business district), "The Limbs" (the canal and main streets), "The Mind & The Soul" (schools and churches)—but I couldn't maintain the analogy and other titles are flat and straightforward. All the small square black and white photos were taken with my Kodak Hawkeye camera in 1961, the year after I graduated from high school, the year before I went off to college. There seem to have been few sunny days that year, at least not on the mornings I went out for pictures, but looming overcast skies seem appropriate for the aimless uncertainty of the life I was living.

On the May morning this photo of the Lockport Locks of the Erie Canal was taken, I rose before dawn, dressed quietly, and left my parents and siblings asleep to walk downtown. I intended to photograph my hometown before it rose from its slumbers—only one image captures someone else out on the street and only a few show vehicles in motion. I hoped my pictures would record something essential about the city, though I couldn't have explained what might have been. Maybe I still can't.

The Erie Canal runs through the center of town at a northeast to southwest angle. Its system of locks, which gave the city its name, allowed vessels to scale or descend the Niagara Escarpment there, bound west to Lake Erie or east to the Hudson River. We lived in a neighborhood to the south of the canal, where all the schools I went to were and where most of my relatives lived, except for my father's father, who lived just north of the canal, on Niagara Street. Our churches, St. Patrick's for my mother's side of the family and her children, First Presbyterian for my father and his father, were also on the north side. On Wednesdays I would walk or bike from school on the south end of town and cross the Big Bridge to reach St. Pat's for religious instruction from nuns who lived in the convent nearby. The primary business district paralleled the canal to the south from its eastern end, crossed it on the Big Bridge, and extended a little further on the north side. Some Sundays, my father would take my sister, my brother, and me downtown to get comic books and the Sunday paper at Kipp's Cigar Store, maybe have a treat at the Crystal, a soda shop, and cross Main Street to stand on the bridge to watch the canal for boats being raised or lowered in the locks. In May 1961, when I took that photo from the Big Bridge, the locks looked serene in dawnlight.

I reached that intersection that morning in time to see the sun sitting in the middle of Main Street, lighting up buildings on both sides of the street. Eventually I walked several blocks of Main Street east, past four five-and-tens, the men's clothing store where my father worked, a department store where I would work the next two summers, another soda shop, and a movie theater, ending near the public library and a final ice cream parlor. Then I veered off down Market Street, one of the main streets linking the prosperous business area at the top of the locks with the rundown shops and tenement blocks of Lowertown. A railroad trestle rose high above the canal and crossed Market Street near the top of the hill. Instead of walking the footbridge that hung from the side of the trestle, familiar to me from boyhood play, I clambered onto the tracks for a more elevated view in either direction. I took one photo looking up the canal, its skyline lined with the backs of business buildings on Main Street, glimmers of canal water far below in the right hand corner, the locks all but missing from the shot; I took another pointed toward Lowertown, the canal at the center narrowing toward the horizon, three bridges growing smaller in the distance, the low level of the water revealing some spits of sediment, the buildings of Lowertown lining the canal indistinct and camouflaged by trees. The camera's single focus never recorded the items in the image that had caught my attention.

Lowertown then was not simply the area below the locks, lining the canal's approach from the east. It was lower in income, lower in upkeep, lower in expectations for its residents. It was as if Lockport was the city on the escarpment that the locks rose to and Lowertown was barely a part of it, something out of sight and out of mind unless you drove down Market Street into the heart of it and passed people milling around in front of the Rage Bar and Grill.

By 1961, of course, the canal's role in migration and commerce was over, but it still flowed through my city and its locks were still at the center of the business district, hidden behind high buildings. I wouldn't have been aware then of the changes to come, especially the ravages of urban renewal soon to neuter the downtown business district or the eventual collapse of the automobile industry, which undermined the city's largest employer. I was an unemployed high school graduate with time on his hands, making cheap thematic albums out of photographs piled in an old cigar-box. My images of Lowertown, while not notable, are now historic. In the intervening decades all of what lined the canal there has been leveled and landscaped into a narrow park between water and road. Most of the businesses I knew on Main Street—the department store, my father's menswear store, the bank my mother worked at, Newberry's, Woolworth's, Grant's, Kresge's—are all gone, and a large retirement complex takes up the opposite side of the block.

Of the locks themselves, the mechanical structure for which the town was named, the early nineteenth century engineering feat that made it possible, even necessary, for there to be any kind of Lockport at all, I have only two photos taken that morning all those decades ago. One from the east end shows mostly a water-filled lock, too close up; the one taken from the Big Bridge shows the west

132

end of the locks from too far away. Nothing stirs within or around them. They remind me how easy it was to cross the canal on those bridges with little awareness that the locks lay below. When I took those pictures, I was the only one walking on either bridge.

How haphazard, it seems to me now, that these pictures were ever taken. How little I understood of what I was seeing or of what had come before those structures existed, of what history lay behind them. How stable and permanent all that seemed in the moments I framed those images. How transient it all turned out to be.

SELF

PHOTOGRAPH

This image of me arrived in an email from my son with this note: "Mom is at a class reunion and found this guy in one of her yearbooks." She was celebrating the fiftieth anniversary of her college graduation. It's a photograph of a photograph of me, one I have no memory of ever seeing. My fiftieth anniversary was the following year; I didn't attend, in spite of the chance to track down the photo on site—I didn't want to break my record of nonattendance.

Eventually I uploaded the photo onto my laptop screen, opposite a Roz Chast cartoon of an "Inside-of-Body-Experience," a woman sitting up in bed thinking, "Once again, here I am." It captures my morning mood too often. It also makes me wonder what kind of inside-of-body-experience the college student in the yearbook picture is undergoing.

I've never seen a caption for the photo and so have no idea what it's meant to record or what yearbook it might be in. Since I'm smoking (probably a Lucky Strike—I stopped smoking over fifty years ago), it wasn't taken in a classroom and from the nearness of someone's shoulder on the edge of the picture it might have been at a meeting of some kind, perhaps for the *Lamron,* our college newspaper ("normal" spelled backwards—it was a teacher's college when I started there) to which I contributed a column and occasional articles, or for *The Experimentalist,* the college literary magazine, of which I was co-editor one year. It likely wasn't a social event; I seem too serious, too intent on what's happening in front of me.

What does the photo tell me about this guy? The slicked-back hair on the side of his head dates him somewhat and the bouncy curls on top undermine a potential commitment to a full D.A. The button-down collar and plaid shirt make a statement about his taste in clothing, one I'm aware he hasn't outgrown. His furrowed forehead suggests a certain level of concentration or attention or concern, as does the angle of his head and his raised eyes. He seems pretty serious and attentive, youthful but almost grown-up.

In my undergraduate years I spent a great deal of time trying to be a writer. I don't know if the caption for the photo indicates that that's who I thought I was. Given the confusions and missteps and follies of those years, I don't mind having the person in this photograph be the one recorded in the yearbook.

*   *   *

Trying to establish a context for that photo sets a chain of impulses and memories in motion. I can't be precise about the time and place it was taken, but rusty synapses are opening—their creaking occasionally heightens my tinnitus. My wife and I have been cleaning out our garage, leafing through boxes of mementoes and books and file folders filled with evidence of long, busy careers. A couple boxes are crammed with folders and binders storing drafts of my writing: high school papers, college papers, short stories, poems, plays, some with comments from various teachers; other boxes hold copies of my journals and notebooks and copies of magazines and academic journals I published in. I have a lot of paper to go through.

What I've scanned sometimes seems familiar, a title of a short story ("The Albatross," "Agnes Dunrose's Hobby"), the start of a mystery novel (*The Graves of Academe*), but sometimes it seems so unfamiliar I wonder whether the draft is mine. I once wrote a novel, *David Gable,* around 96 pages of youthful melodrama, sometime around the end of high school, maybe in the two years before I started college. It may be in an as-yet-unopened box somewhere but probably succumbed to mold in a damp basement years ago. All that early writing makes me recall a character in Fitzgerald's *Tender Is the Night* joking about "the Juvenalia [sic] of my collected editions" and the scholarly attention given to Jane Austen's *Juvenilia,* written between the ages of ten and seventeen. I consider my material to be my "literary remains," like my grandmother's newspaper column and unfinished novel, my father's few poems, the diaries and journals and letters of the people I've written about in the past.

And just as I've hoped to get to know those people through their often unguarded writing, I've wondered who I would find in the pages of that writing in those boxes. What would those efforts at creative writing reveal about that guy in the photograph, the one who, no matter what uncertainty I have about what he's doing there, I am certain thought of himself at that time as a writer.

SOME MORNINGS

Some mornings, after waking, I lie in bed, eyes closed, on my back, stretched out as if in savasana, covers to my chin, and try to think what I will do this day. I try not to think of chores, like making the bed and emptying the dishwasher and making coffee as I do each morning, like doing laundry as I do each Sunday or putting out the trash and the recycling as I do each Friday. I try not to remember what writing packets I need to critique or what webpages I need to check for online postings, what emails I should reply to or what meetings I should attend. I try to focus on what I will do that will satisfy me that I am doing something I need to do for myself. Those mornings I get no further than this, avoiding what I don't want to think about and clearing my mind for what I do want to think about, preparing space for what I most need to think about.

And nothing happens. That space is empty. Nothing comes to mind, nothing comes into my mind, nothing emerges from my mind.

On those mornings it doesn't take so long to arrive at empty space. I think: I will lie here and think of what I must do, and when nothing appears I think again: I will lie here and think of what I must do, and when still nothing appears I think the same thought again, again and again, until I give up and rise and make the bed and dress and, being sure to have turned on the computer in my study before I go downstairs, make my coffee and empty the dishwasher, and bring my coffee upstairs, type in my password, delete the spam on my email account, check the weather, check my list of things to do, and begin to think about which thing I tried not to think about that I should do first. Some mornings it takes awhile to decide.

Sometimes I sense something else I must do for myself but can't determine what it must be. Sometimes I forget to wonder until I wake the next morning and lie in bed, eyes closed, on my back, as if in savasana, and try to think what I will do this day.

> Summer Solstice morning—
> shadow puppet birds
> flash across the blinds

137

MEMORY

Music when soft voices die
Vibrates in the memory
—Percy Bysshe Shelley

It began to rain around midnight. In occasional moments of semi-wakefulness throughout the rest of the night I heard it beat against the windows and the siding on the garage. It was constant, persistent, regular. When I rose, just before dawn, the sky growing lighter, the rain growing lighter, I peered through the blinds at the glistening driveway and street and patches of lawn. I could see raindrops plashing softly in puddles.

Then I thought that these were April showers I'd been hearing and, before I could even acknowledge to myself that I'd had that thought, I was hearing the song in my head. "Though April showers may come your way,/ they bring the flowers that bloom in May,/ so if it's raining, have no regrets,/ because it isn't raining rain, you know,/ it's raining violets." The song didn't stop with the first verse but, as I stood there, it played in my mind all the way through—I waited for it to finish before I left the window. I recognized the inflections and intonations of Al Jolson's recording, the one I'd first heard my mother play in my childhood, the one I'd played on my own Jolson albums decades later. For a little while I stood smiling out at the rain, listening to the song playing in my head. Later in the day I sang it out loud all the way through as I strolled in sunshine to the mailbox, sang it alone in the car on the way to the supermarket and also on the way back.

Nothing extraordinary in this, of course. Particularly in spring, when I notice robins again, I'm apt to launch into "When the red, red robin comes bob, bob, bobbin' along," usually trying to imitate Jolson's performance. Some mornings I wake up with a song from the previous day's cardio class in the background of my consciousness, Taylor Swift's "Shake It Off" for example, or Elvis's "Bossa Nova Baby," or the Zac Brown Band's "Where the Boat Leaves From." You know how a song can stick with you through the day. But whenever those tunes replay themselves on an automatic loop in my brain, they've been triggered by my having recently heard the recordings. Looking out at the rain I might have thought of "Rhythm of the Rain" by the Cascades or "Raindrops" by Dee Clark or "Rain on the Roof" by the Lovin' Spoonful, recordings that come into my head only now, through a deliberate search for examples. But this was different. What would make me aware that it was April when I rose? Why did that song seem to be poised at the threshold of my consciousness, waiting for me to open the blind and behold the rain?

There's something here I don't understand about memory. It's as if memory—my memory—has a separate existence housed somewhere in my subconscious. Most of the time it seems passive, a repository of images and sounds and language dormant until roused to life by my will—my conscious effort to recall items of information (what was that song about the rhythm of the rain? who recorded "Raindrops"? what did the cover of my mother's Jolson album look like?) But here memory seemed active, even assertive, insisting that I pay attention to something I hadn't thought about for years and years. As if *it* decided this was a good occasion to bring forward something long neglected but still present, still stored, impossible to discard.

Who's in charge here, me or my memory? What else has it ambushed me with, made me remember without warning? I'm not complaining, you understand. "April Showers" was a pretty pleasant memory to be surprised with. It set me off later in the day and in the days that followed remembering other Jolson songs on those records, Jolson performances on film, Larry Parks as Jolson in *The Jolson Story* and *Jolson Sings Again*. Generally cheerful, lively songs. Some of them I sang to myself, tentatively imitating Jolson's mannerisms. It could have been worse. Sometimes, I'm sure, it has been.

I don't particularly want to call those worse memories to mind, the ones that arise in a cloud of embarrassment or guilt, the ones that revive past sorrows, past regrets. They come too easily as it is, surface unannounced, make me chastise my mirror image with rude gestures from both hands. And yet there are perfectly benign memories that won't come at all, harmless little memories, contented memories, memories I should be happy to relive. No matter how earnestly I cup my chin in my hand and scowl and snort huffily, wherever those memories are stored they remain hidden, inaccessible behind sealed and unmarked synapses. Only later will some of them surface unexpectedly, when no longer needed, as if reluctantly emerging from hibernation. I'm sure they're all there, all the memories that make me blush or make me beam, all the memories I made no effort to store, all the ones I never want to lose, but my memory won't provide a guidebook to let me master access to them, decide which ones are always on call, which ones should enter a mental cryogenic state.

Each morning when I rise from my bed I separate slats on the blind to look out on the day, see if there are lights on in the condos across the street, locate where the sun will rise or has risen, try to intuit how the day will be. No songs about pleasant weather arise unbidden—only now do I think of "Blue Skies" or "It's a Good Day," the Bing Crosby versions, but that's a deliberate search. I want to pay attention and notice when memory springs something on me, figure out how often this happens. I want to be able to predict what my memory might have in store.

*   *   *

> *It's a poor sort of memory that only works backwards.*
> —Lewis Carroll

Throughout the years that I was growing up a large portrait photograph of a woman hung in our living room, on the same wall as a photo of my mother in her wedding dress. When one of my siblings or I would ask who the woman in the picture was, my mother or father would explain that she was our grandmother, our father's mother, and that she had died a while ago. This helped explain why the portrait of someone we didn't know would have such a pride of place in our home. Over time we remembered who she was and could remind one another if any of us forgot, but all we knew about her was her name and her relationship to my father. Her portrait still hung on the wall after my parents divorced, and it continued to hang there after my mother died and my father moved back into the house to care for my youngest sister. Years later, after my father died, the photo was bequeathed to me. When I unwrapped it, I stared for a long time at my grandmother's face, searching for my father's features there.

140

Since then I've learned quite a bit about her by what artifacts I could find of her life—her short-lived newspaper column on personality, her unfinished novel, a handwritten note or letter, a half dozen or so photos taken over her lifetime. I've tried to read and write my way into a sense of knowing her, fully aware that it will not be the same as if I knew her in life. And as I struggle to do this, I keep reminding myself that, in fact, our lives briefly overlapped. She died the day after my fifth birthday. In those five years we lived in the same town, less than a dozen blocks apart. She must have known me—I was her first-born grandchild, for a while her only grandchild. My father, serving in the Marines when I was born, was home the Christmas after my first birthday; he and my mother and I must have driven across town from my maternal grandparents' house, where my mother and I lived, to my paternal grandparents' house in that holiday season. Photographs confirm that my father and I were together that Christmas, when I was thirteen months old, but none records either of us with his parents.

I can imagine reasons my grandmother and I might have been apart, knowing now about her health and her repeated need to find more hospitable climates for her asthma, knowing now about my mother's behavior in the years my father was gone. But my father was home for the last two years of her life. Surely in those 1,826 days she and I were simultaneously alive, we spent some time together; surely in the roughly 730 days that measured the end of her time in my father's life, he and I would have visited her.

At one time I must have had a memory of being with her, but no such memory has ever surfaced.

There are ways of prompting memories to return. If I look at a photo of the house I grew up in, I can wander all through it, all around it, out into the neighborhood, retrace the walks to schools and playgrounds. When I draw a map of my hometown on a chalkboard, modeling a prompt for students, I immediately start playing memory videos of being in parts of it.

And so I revisit in memory my grandmother's home, where my grandfather lived after her death, where my father's stepmother lives still. I picture the layout of the rooms, some vague fragments of décor. I recall at once a Christmas visit, with my father's relatives milling around and my mother paying attention to children rather than engaging with adults; I was old enough to notice my mother's distance from others, but don't know how old. It was years after my grandmother's death. I can wander some of the rooms in memory, recognize people in my father's family, but can't pin down when I saw them or even be sure I saw them there. I visualize walking down a hall to the bedroom where coats might sometimes be piled on the bed or where a weary child might rest until his parents were ready to go home. I foggily envision the bed and begin to wonder if once I saw a frail older woman sitting up in it. The harder I concentrate on clarifying the scene, the less certain I am that I'm not confusing it with another such scene in another house in another town. I can't be sure I'm not imagining the scene, willing it to transform into a memory.

No doubt I've lost a great many memories over the years, ones I wasn't attentive enough to hang on to, ones I feel no regrets over losing because I don't know what they were. But sometimes I wake out of dreams aware that I've been wrestling with my memory, urging it to release what has to be stored there, let me relive even a single moment my grandmother and I must have shared.

It's perversely paradoxical—that memory will not let me forget things I don't want to remember and yet won't let me recall something that seems so vital to me, not simply an image of the portrait that hung on our living room wall but a feeling for the living presence of the woman who gazed out of the frame.

*   *   *

Preserve your memories, they're all that's left you.
—Paul Simon

The other day in the shower an image flashed into my mind, one of those vivid images from the past, perhaps prompted by a song playing in my head unbidden or by a chance phrase that came up in my wife's conversation. Perhaps it was one of those things that recur in memory because of repetition—you use an old coffee mug and remember who gave it to you and where you got it, which leads you to remember other moments with that person or those people or in that place or at that time or under those circumstances—what led up to the moment that you got that mug—and a string of memories you haven't asked to access and images you haven't tried to project on the screen of your consciousness rush across your mind. Sometimes you remember having conjured that image on other occasions when you used that mug or when you inadvertently prompted that memory, so that the surfacing of that image isn't exactly predictable but it no longer surprises you when it shows up. Usually this kind of thing flits across and dissolves and vanishes—I've already forgotten what image flashed then and which morning it was—but I do remember standing in the shower and thinking for the first time: When I'm dead, all of those images will cease to flash anywhere in the universe; all those memories, whether clear or unclear or accurate or not, will be stored nowhere. My computer's hard drive will have more of my memories in texts and images, including the ones I deleted, than my own brain will have, and they will be harder to erase than it was to erase the images and events and experiences stored willingly or unwillingly in my actual physical—is it physical?—mind.

And while all my handwritten journals and typed manuscripts will continue to record my edited perceptions and my proofread memories until they're recycled, long before they're gone I will have been composted entirely. I've only just now thought of that—the triumph of journaling over deliberate cognition—but have to remind myself that's not the thought I had in the shower that morning.

That thought was this: it's not only all the images and memories in *my* mind that will vanish entirely from existence—to the degree that memories and images in the mind have existence—all the images and memories of everyone who dies anywhere and everywhere in the world each day will vanish entirely as well. If I add up all that's stored and apparently haphazardly catalogued in my mind and memory and multiply that figure by the number of individuals who cease to be alive anywhere and everywhere on the planet in a single day—a single year, a single decade—how many images and memories have evaporated beyond any possibility of retrieval? All those hours and days and weeks and years of accumulating those images and memories—what exactly were they for, if they can be so instantaneously non-existent? The scale of loss appalls and astonishes me; so too does the likelihood that the answer to what they were for is, *They weren't for anything*.

And now, when I take a shower, in addition to the other unbidden images and memories that crop up in my mind, the memory of this recognition of mortality and its losses is likely to crop up as well. If I deliberately step into the shower repeating a cheery song lyric or percolating a response to something my wife said, perhaps my memory will bypass the synapse that replays that epiphany. Otherwise, opening the shower curtain is drawing back a veil of ephemerality, making me feel that I bathe in impermanence, in the evanescence of soap suds and shampoo circling the drain, in the insubstantial vapor of steam, in the transience of memory.

MIRRORS

At night, when I am propped up reading or watching television, I glance at the mirror on the dresser opposite the foot of our bed. I catch myself leaning to my right, the mirror image's left, and I straighten my posture, make sure my shoulders are level with one another. We've owned the dresser for twenty years or more, but it's been opposite the foot of our bed for only four; I've now seen us sitting against the pillows piled against the wall for over a thousand nights. Sometimes, when I'm the only one upright in the mirror, I wonder who I'm seeing.

> In mirror image
> the face I think is mine
> unknown to the world

When, in *The Tale of Genji*, the hero Genji is about to travel away from his wife Murasaki, they each write a tanka in which they hope his image will never leave her mirror. That images might endure in a mirror haunts me. My wife's mirror and dresser used to be my mother's, purchased in the early days of my parents' first marriage to one another. In my mother's bedroom it stood opposite the foot of her bed. How often did my mother and father discover themselves in that mirror? How often did her second husband see himself there? When my parents married each other a second time and moved their bedroom downstairs—the bedroom now was mine and mirrorless— the dresser was positioned off to the side and the mirror reflected only the inadvertent presence of my father and the daily visit of my mother to her dresser drawers. My mother would have stooped before them as now my wife does each day, glanced in the mirror as she straightened, barely noticed herself crossing in front of it. Who did my mother see in the mirror in the nearly thirty years it was hers? Who have we seen in the decades it's been ours? If I look hard enough, will I find images of my mother, my father, my very temporary stepfather, even my younger self in the mirror?

> The three way mirror
> in my father's clothing store—
> me and not me side by side by side

Marriage, Joan Didion writes in *The Year of Magical Thinking*, encompasses not only memory and time but "also, paradoxically, the denial of time." In a marriage you see yourself through your partner's eyes each day and gain no perspective on the passage of time; only after her husband's death ends forty years of marriage and she begins to see herself through the eyes of other people does Didion realize she is not still twenty-nine. Just so. Once I thought I saw my long-dead father in the background of a recent photograph and only slowly recognized that it was I who held his shoulders and arms that way, who bent to just that angle, who projected just that purposeful stride. It made me begin to interrogate my mirrors, which hadn't mentioned how time was passing. Often now I wake without expecting to see the face I saw in the mirror the night before; it will be a face I know but is not mine, not a twenty-nine year old, not the forty-year old my wife married, not whomever I expected to see. I check the mirror from time to time throughout the day to see if I have shown up yet.

> Grandfather's face
> in the morning mirror—
> mine emerges later

RAIN

Our children and grandchildren are up to their knees in the waves before we notice the dark cloud above the lake, a blur of rain below it, moving toward us. As I wade out to them, the cloud comes closer, and we return to the beach. Within minutes the sky darkens overhead and the first chilly raindrops strike bare shoulders and backs. Under towels wrapped around us, token protection against the rain, we huddle together while other bathers retreat, leaving us alone at the water's edge in the rain. Then I see my granddaughter, the ten-year-old, still standing in breaking waves and falling rain, smiling at us, shrugging nonchalantly, never flinching.

Heavy raindrops punctuate the water around her and dapple the beach around us, sudden shocks on our shoulders, sudden speckling of lake water, sudden round depressions in sand. We stand and withstand and watch the clearing sky beyond the cloud and hope to wait out the rain. And we do. It passes over my granddaughter and then over the beach, no longer dimples the sand around us, floats off inland, and we feel the sun's warmth again. Soon I am as deep into the lake as my granddaughter was, and her siblings and cousins are wading in, and my granddaughter is swimming, still aware of how she alone withstood what we all retreated from, unaware of how she looked, alone in the lake, smiling in the rain.

In Wisconsin, when I enter her house and call hello, my granddaughter Lilly, nearly three, shouts "Grandpa!" and runs laughing to clasp my knees; I lift her up and her arms encircle my neck and we squeeze one another. In Florida, a few days later, as I step out of the guest room, my granddaughter Eliza, nearly two, sees me and smiles and runs from the kitchen to hug my knees; it's the first time she's done this and as I lift her, I try to smile at her mother without letting my eyes fill with tears.

I feel these moments as blessings but think of them as synchronicity, moments in a juxtaposition that tells me to pay attention. A synchronicity is a coincidence of events that feels meaningful to the person experiencing them, even if that person doesn't know why they feel meaningful.

*   *   *

Cheryl Strayed starts Part Five of *Wild* with a quote from Mary Oliver's poem, "The Summer Day": "Tell me, what is it you plan to do/ with your one wild and precious life?" It startled me when I read it. The epigraph is appropriate enough for that section of the memoir, but it set off a diverting series of reverberations in me.

I'd first encountered those lines decades before, in the emails of a friend with whom I'd once been intimate. It had been a recurring quote below her signature. Each time I'd read it, it seemed a pertinent question. I soon found the quote in emails from other friends and acquaintances, as if I'd blundered into a far-flung community of like-minded people, generous and encouraging, eager to offer inspiration. At first the power of the lines was enhanced by the deep affection I felt for that friend, but over time they read to me like a haiku or like a Zen koan, something that made you pause and consider whether you were rewarding your spirit with the choices you were making, with what you were doing with your life.

Once or twice I wondered if I too should have a tagline for my emails, likely something from Thoreau. The first that came to mind, "We live meanly, like ants: our lives are frittered away in detail," struck me at once as less uplifting than Oliver's lines. The other Thoreau quote that stayed in my head was closer in spirit to hers: "I went to the woods because I wished to live deliberately and not, when I came to die, discover that I had not lived at all." Thoreau reminds us of a limit on the time we have. So, it turns out, does Oliver. In the line that precedes the closing lines of "The Summer Day," she asks, "Doesn't everything die at last, and too soon?" No one wondering "what you plan to do/ with your one wild and precious life" had quoted that line before it, which adds a note of urgency to the planning.

Who we are and where we are in our lives affects the way we read all literature. When I encountered Oliver's quote again in *Wild,* I was surprised to be startled. In decades past I had smiled fondly and nodded sagely each time I read it, but nowadays I tend more to ponder how deliberately I've lived and what I'm likely to discover when I come to die. Nowadays I'm more aware that everything dies at last—"and too soon." Instead of asking ourselves what we plan to do, perhaps a time comes when the question should be, "What *have you done* with your one wild and precious life?"

I liked the question better when my options were open and I hadn't already chosen between those roads diverging in the dark wood in the middle of my life's journey (to completely muddle my poetic references). In truth, I often read that epigraph in light of the lost friendship of the person who introduced me to it, a loss in large degree my fault. And so I read it now with twinges of regret, and all my regrets begin to pool around it and rise to the surface. Surely Oliver didn't mean the poem to be accusatory; surely my life hasn't entirely been missteps and mistakes.

Granted, my one life hasn't been wild; it's been ploddingly productive in a modest, largely unobtrusive way, and easy to plan, following academic calendars and publishing deadlines and conference dates. Not so much living deliberately as living—what? complacently? placidly? In "The Summer Day" the narrator's comments are prompted by intimations that her activity—calmly holding her palm open while a grasshopper feeds from it—isn't a significant use of her time. But what makes our limited lives precious may be just such unplanned and spontaneous moments.

Like the moments when my granddaughters rush up to hug my knees. How can I account for the unplanned blessing of those moments? How can I not be humbly grateful for them? If I put them on one side of the scales, I find I can lighten the weight of regrets on the other side.

But I didn't know this at once after encountering the Oliver quote again. It was something synchronicity and my granddaughters had to teach me.

*   *   *

The songs my granddaughters and I perform together are generations old; the most familiar versions date back before my birth. I learned those lyrics in their parents' childhoods, lyrics their parents also have sung with them. In my childhood did anyone ever sing them to me—ever invite me to sing along? Tradition depends on bringing something out of the past into the present and passing it on to the future, whether you're aware that that's what you're doing or not. Inadvertence doesn't automatically diminish the value of what you carry on. If my great-great-grandchildren have these songs sung to them, neither they nor even their parents or grandparents may recognize themselves as carrying on a relatively minor tradition.

In Florida, Eliza, now two, lets me push her in a swing attached to a tree in her front yard and listens to me sing. When I get to the end of lines in "The Wheels on the Bus" I hear her quietly echo the last words—"round and round," "swish, swish, swish," "shh, shh, shh." When I sing "Itsy Bitsy Spider" she indistinctly mutters some of the lyrics and I see her hands moving, fingers wiggling for the spider's climb up the waterspout, the rain coming down, the sun coming out, the spider climbing again. She smiles and looks at my hands, expecting me to do the finger motions with her, and laughs when I do.

In Wisconsin, a few days later, Lilly, now three, sits with me at the counter island in her kitchen, finishing her lunch. She asks me to sing and after a couple Nursery Rhymes I start "The Wheels on the Bus," which she knows well. Her fingers wag back and forth like the wipers on the bus and she holds two forefingers to her lips for the shushing. She asks for "Itsy Bitsy Spider" and readies her hands for the finger motions, singing along with me and with her eyes encouraging me to do the hand gestures too. She smiles approvingly as I raise my fingers.

Maybe the question to ask at the end is: Acknowledging that you have regrets, are you content with what you've done with your one wild and precious life? Happily enough, I am not startled to find that I am.

A PERCEIVABLE SOUL

The last time we saw her, two weeks before she died, her dementia seemed to have taken everything from her. The traits we thought particularly hers were no longer visible to us. We could discern nothing of her intelligence, her compassion, her vitality, her humor, her charm. Physically and mentally, she'd been reduced to her barest essentials, virtually immobile, inarticulate, non-communicative, inexpressive except through the intensity of her gaze. In my mind my brother-in-law had become a widower while his wife still lived. He had lost her and she had lost herself and he knew and surely, somehow, she knew that she wouldn't come back. Before long, her physical existence would end, but already her personality had vanished. It was hard to know what still functioned in her mind, how much she still knew who she was, still knew what was happening to her. She seemed to have been reduced to the core of her existence.

But, watching them from her doorway that morning, we saw him stand smiling at the foot of her bed, gazing raptly at her, we saw her gaze fixed on him, and we realized something about the nature of love. We couldn't recognize the person we had known in the woman before him, but her husband could. He could still see her essence, and, mutely, she seemed to know it. Though so much had vanished, for him, her soul was still perceivable, and he still welcomed the sight of it.

wake /wāk/
noun (1) a watch or a vigil before a burial
(2) a track or path left behind; an aftermath
phrase "in the wake of": as a result or consequence of;
following the same path

When her daughter put her on the line, my sister declared almost at once: "I'm dying." She'd been told she'd have a few months before the cancer took her. I promised to get back home for a final visit, but about a week and a half later she was gone. My wife and I came east for her wake and my brother and his wife came north and her children came back to our hometown from where they now lived. After years apart I slowly recognized her three sons and two daughters and, by family resemblances, could almost identify some of her grandchildren, now adults and parents themselves,. Other relatives I hadn't seen for decades came to the wake—cousins who had already lost one parent and one sibling, a widowed aunt, a widowed step-grandmother. I was suddenly aware of how much I'd fallen out of touch with all these people I'd grown up with, how little I'd understood their losses over recent years. I couldn't grasp my own sense of loss but most of them knew at once what I was feeling. My sister was not the first of our generation to leave us, but she was the first of my siblings. Beyond private bursts of grief I couldn't figure out how to respond to her passing.

None of the hard moments my sister and I had shared surfaced in memory, though I knew we'd had them. Maybe the presence of her descendants made me remember how we'd compare notes during our infrequent long-distance calls. When I marveled that my oldest granddaughter had become a teenager and that two grandsons were poised to make that shift, my sister mentioned recently welcoming her fifth great-grandchild. We thought it funny that I was so much older and yet so far behind in terms of progeny. At her wake I saw how many there were to mourn her, to share—and hold on to—their memories of her.

Mention in my sister's obituary of her fondness for Elvis Presley reminded me of her collection of recordings and memorabilia, something we used to joke about. I remembered how, in 1960, we both went to the earliest showing of *G. I. Blues*, Presley's first film after his army stint, at the Palace Theatre. When it ended and I went home, she stayed, viewed every showing that day, and went to see it again the next day. She was then fourteen years old. Over time, partly in defiance of our kidding, she stayed loyal to Elvis.

I remembered too that there were no consequences to her coming home late from a day-long movie binge, perhaps because our mother was the first one to buy Elvis's recordings and play them on the phonograph in our living room. My sister's fandom went far beyond my mother's—Mom also played Glenn Miller, Harry James, Frank Sinatra, Bing Crosby, Spike Jones, Stan Freberg, Rosemary Clooney, eventually Johnny Cash and Roger Miller—but my mother let us watch *Your Hit Parade* and *American Bandstand* and danced around the living room with us. There was often music in our house.

My sister and our younger brother both married and became parents before I did and all their children were born before my mother died. I'm sure some of them remembered her—she was pretty attentive to her grandchildren. She missed out on their growing up and on the great-grandchildren she would have loved to meet. At my sister's wake I remembered a family event where our mother's absence was palpable to both of us.

When my brother's daughter married her longtime boyfriend, it was a milestone event. The wedding reception was at a hall in our hometown. There was my younger brother as the father of the bride, which I wouldn't be for many more years, and there were my father and my stepmother and a couple of uncles and aunts chatting quietly at the long tables. With plenty of raucous moves, the wedding party started dancing to tunes of the times, what was groovy in the late 1980s, and none of my generation or the generation before felt able to join it. But then the D.J. started playing earlier periods of pop music, songs more familiar to older generations, and the younger dancers began dropping out as their elders stepped onto the dance floor.

My sister and I joined in for some of the numbers, especially those I remembered twisting or ponying to in college, but when the musical era dropped back to the forties, to our parents' generation of swing, the two of us found ourselves alone on the dance floor, comfortably jitterbugging to a tune like "Boogie Woogie Bugle

Boy" by the Andrews Sisters or "Chattanooga Choo-Choo" by the Glenn Miller Band. We knew those songs; we knew how to dance to them from dancing with our mother in our living room. We'd seen her dancing with our uncle at earlier family wedding receptions and reunions, where he'd also polkaed with their mother and she'd polkaed with her uncles. My sister and I danced together with confidence, with familiarity, with energy and delight, laughing often at near missteps. At some point, I believe, my sister and I both simultaneously knew that something had shifted between generations—there we were behaving like our parents' generation—and there were our children—at least my sister's and my brother's—occupying the space our generation had been in such a short time ago. We were suddenly in new roles and overjoyed to be in them. It was as if our family genes had got the better of us. We couldn't be more pleased with who we were at that moment, smiling, laughing, swinging each other around, moving as we remembered our mother and her youngest brother moving.

At my sister's wake, among people sharing memories, I told the story of our dancing together and my brother stood near, nodding and laughing hard. He remembered watching us at his daughter's reception. The vision of my sister and me boogieing alone on the dance floor was as fresh for him as it had continued to be for us over the years. Still smiling, I made my way alone to where my sister lay and then gazed at her through tears. I wanted to remind her of our dancing together that day, hear again her laughter as when we'd recalled it in the past. I wanted her to know that I still knew what it meant to us to share the memory of following in our mother's wake.

EXISTENCE

I don't exist. I'm not even here. I don't exist.
Birdman (Or the Unexpected Virtue of Ignorance)

Obscure (probably) but not wholly invisible (he's surprised
by the difference between "obscure" and "invisible").
He's finally obtained obscurity.
Michael Cunningham, *The Snow Queen*

The first time I saw it, I didn't laugh at Jeremy Nguyen's obscurity cartoon in *The New Yorker,* just nodded, smiled wryly, and snorted a short "ha." I showed it to my wife along with one by Roz Chast about "Life Before Caller I.D.," echoing our grudge against telemarketing calls, and one by Emily Flake where two priests hold their stomachs and one admits eating "a whole sleeve of communion wafers." She laughed at Chast and Flake, gave Nguyen a slight smile, and turned back to making breakfast, but for the rest of the week I looked at the Nguyen every day. I didn't laugh or smile those times, just gazed at the picture and reread the caption, and finally downloaded the image to my laptop.

In Nguyen's cartoon, a middle-aged man sprawls on his study floor, head and shoulders raised with apparent effort, looking towards the viewer. The caption reads, "Help! I've fallen into obscurity and I can't get up!" The exclamation points give the words a plaintive air. It's a play on the Life Alert commercials, the ones where a fallen elderly woman hears a voice on her medical alarm pendant reassuring her that help is on the way. What gives Nguyen's cartoon its edge is the sense that the man's situation is psychological, not physical—he is in danger only of mounting self-pity; no one will offer consolation. Most viewers likely find him comically pathetic and self-dramatizing. I kinda felt that way too.

But—

Anyone can tell by the setting that the man is a writer. A large bookcase neatly lined with a variety of volumes rises on one wall and, immediately behind him, near a wide window, stand an empty desk chair and a square table holding a typewriter, a sheet of paper scrolled into it. The typewriter is the vital, telling feature; it identifies not only the plaintive figure's occupation (or perhaps

156

preoccupation) but also his somewhat archaic perspective—a typewriter? not a laptop?—on how a writer operates in the world. The man himself, in that tidy, well-organized setting, seems relatively secure in life—he is no starving artist. His white hair, his glasses, his open shirt collar sticking out of the neck of a sweater or sweatshirt—all these indicate his age and his datedness. The longer I gaze at him lying there the more I suspect that, when he fell into obscurity, he didn't have far to fall.

Probably few readers lingered over this cartoon to deconstruct it to the degree I have. But then, I find myself uncomfortably identifying with the man's situation. I'm hunched over my desk in our study—at a laptop, not a typewriter—before a window facing a row of condos mirroring our own; bookshelves overflow with volumes of various sizes along the side walls. My white hair is still askew after a night's sleep and a brief morning interval uncertain about the need to get up; my cheap reading glasses perch uncomfortably on my nose; I'm dressed in my best sweatpants and matching jacket and newest slippers. Though more comfortable and more colorful than the man on the floor and probably older, I'm drawn to his plight because I sense that I share it. I feel, like him, as if I've fallen into obscurity and can't get up and I wonder how much of a fall it actually was. I look up antonyms for "obscure"—I'm on a laptop after all—and then ask myself how "perceptible," "known," or "apparent" I think I once was.

*　　*　　*

A few years earlier I'd connected in a similar way to the film *Birdman*. The main character, Riggan Thomson, once played the superhero Birdman in a trilogy of popular films (and is played by Michael Keaton, who was Batman in two movies); now he's rehearsing a play he wrote based on Raymond Carver's *What We Talk About When We Talk About Love*. At times he says that he feels as if he no longer exists, that he's disappearing. He means—my interpretation—he no longer knows who he is; when the film role that once defined him evaporated, it carried away his sense of identity. Isn't our sense of who we are determined by the roles we play in the drama of our own lives?

157

So here's the thing: after my son and my wife and I left the theater, I waited until she and I were alone to confess that I was struck by the times the main character repeated things I'd said recently about myself. My wife replied, noncommittally, "Yes, I noticed that." We both caught Riggan's remarks about disappearing, and both were aware of how, a few years after I retired, fuming about my constant glumness, I'd said aloud, more than once, that I hadn't retired, I'd vanished—I'd disappeared.

Riggan is so identifiable that, when he inadvertently runs through Times Square in his underwear, passers-by salute him and want his autograph and ask him to pose with them in their selfies. I have no similar standing in any one's mind, including my own. Over a long career, first as a high school English teacher, then as a university professor, and continuously as a writer, I've been fairly inconspicuous. A detached observer might reasonably ask, how does a largely invisible entity disappear?

As an attached observer, I ask myself: Where did this sense of having disappeared come from? What sense of myself in the world did I once have that I no longer have?

*   *   *

As a working teacher among students and colleagues, I never questioned my presence in the world. I continually engaged in earnest enterprises that absorbed my attention: classes, conferences, publications. When I retired from the university where I'd spent most of my career and moved to where my wife would redirect hers, I concentrated on launching or completing projects as if I were still that preoccupied professor. It took awhile to realize that, despite my busywork, I was largely isolated in between my wife's morning and evening commute. After we moved again, I joined the faculty of a low-residency MFA program where, except for a two-week summer residency, I communicated only online with students and, occasionally, faculty—interactive but invisible. It was intermittently amicable and rewarding and kept my attention away from myself enough, until program mismanagement severed that connection. I felt only temporarily sidelined at first, devoting my uncommitted summer to a long-neglected project, but I soon understood my circumstances better—no deadlines to meet, no insistent email to answer, no responsibilities to attend to. I sometimes worried about my memory—what had I forgotten to do?—until I realized I hadn't forgotten anything; I simply had nothing I had to do.

*   *   *

My constant awareness of synchronicity feels like a low-grade alarm system in my psyche, ever alert for coincidental links to subjects that intermittently prey on my mind. Lately, I've been conscious of celebrity death, especially of someone I've read or viewed or heard my age but preferably older. When Mary Oliver died at 83 I recalled appropriating her lines "Tell me, what is it you plan to do/with your one wild and precious life?" in an essay. When I first read the poem I mildly agreed with the line before them, "Doesn't everything die at last, and too soon?," but gave it little attention; now I'm only too aware of that question. In the same way, when our cardio instructor made us dance to Paul Simon's "Slip Sliding Away," his lyrics stayed in my head for days (*"the nearer your destination/ the more you're slip sliding away"*); I'd ignored the song's darkness when I first heard it years before.

In an article by Mike Pride after the death of his friend Donald Hall at 89—(Hall once told him, "Rumor has it that everyone dies")—I was most struck by Pride's off-hand comment, "After retiring in my sixties, I had experienced a sudden invisibility." It echoed that recurring concern of mine. Pride, former editor of *The Concord Monitor,* was confronted with an unavoidable absence of presence in the familiar world *("I don't exist. I'm not even here."),*

Depending on what retirees do with their days when they no longer do what they did, retirement doesn't always trigger a sense of invisibility. I know former colleagues who turned full-time to hobbies or passions—remodeling automobiles for one, more fervent dedication to his golf game for another; they were still in the world if not in the world where they'd spent decades. People in those new worlds perceived them in their current identities. They were still apparent.

In Michael Cunningham's *The Snow Queen* a musician realizes that finally releasing an album is unlikely to bring him riches and fame, that he will become "obscure (probably) but not

159

wholly invisible"; he finds it reassuring to have "finally obtained obscurity." Consider someone fingering through upright rows of vinyl record albums or CDs in a rack uncertain about who individual artists are or what kind of music they make; consider someone reading the spines of volumes on bookshelves with no recognition of either author or title. To them, those recordings or volumes, no matter how unfamiliar or unidentifiable, are only obscure—they are not invisible.

Some of my books are still in certain libraries, even in certain bookstores. Strangers sometimes see their titles, maybe glance at their covers (The last one had a lovely cover). Perhaps I haven't *fallen* into obscurity; maybe I just don't appreciate how securely I've obtained it.

*   *   *

Nguyen's cartoon figure and Cunningham's musician consider obscurity from different perspectives, but both think the stage below obscurity is equivalent to nonexistence, the kind of disappearance the actor in *Birdman* feels he has undergone, the kind of invisibility the editor experienced after retiring. They make me wonder about my own nagging sense of near-nonexistence. I remember a haunting moment in David Hinton's *Hunger Mountain: A Field Guide to Mind and Landscape* where he claims that "in the moment of perception, there is no 'I' perceiving; there is simply perception, the opening of consciousness . . ." Glimpsing himself in a mirror, he tells us, "[I] gaze at myself, gaze at myself gazing at myself" and he can't tell "what it is that's seeing and what seen." The more deeply he looks into himself, the more the creature he is eludes him. The moment suggests that "we are most fundamentally the opening of consciousness, that gaze of awareness, rather than the center of thought and intention with which we normally identify."

I've experienced such moments gazing at myself in a mirror. I see a figure making blank or dour or silly faces (and sometimes abrupt gestures), but at that moment I don't have a full sense of his (my own) identity, his (my own) actual existence. Clearly I exist— I stand there and feel an ache in my lower back or in my neck or feel my fingernails rake across my skin as I scratch my nose. I *must* exist. I am perceivable; I perceive myself as, if the image were reversed,

160

others must perceive me—my wife, my children and grandchildren, bystanders in the grocery check-out line. But if I look long enough, I can't tell, in Hinton's words, "what it is that is seeing and what seen." My mirror image is as remote from me as if he were a different person, as if he were a stranger. He may be visible, visually familiar, but his identity seems obscure.

I am beginning to understand that the issue is not so much how obscure or invisible I am to other people but how obscure or invisible I am to myself. I remember those moments of uncertainty about who I'm looking at in the mirror—that individual's essential core. Did all that teaching and all that writing divert my attention from coming to terms with myself? If that's the case, then ceasing to teach and concluding long-term writing projects made my identity evaporate, left me with the same physical presence so recognizable in photographs and mirrors but removed the preoccupation with my external identity, the exterior of an unexamined, uncertain interior self. (*"I don't exist. I'm not even here."*) If I knew who I was, I would know what I should be doing. I would take myself for granted. Throughout our lives we are obscure to many and nonexistent to multitudes, but it doesn't trouble us because we are unaware of it, so caught up in an interactive life in which we feel perceivable and apparent. The interaction, the constant involvement, automatically confirms our existence; we never question it until we step away from our external activity. That's when we feel we are disappearing, falling into and beyond obscurity, becoming invisible. We ourselves are the ones who can't see us.

In her classic essay "On Keeping a Notebook," Joan Didion advised us "to keep on nodding terms with the people we used to be, whether we find them attractive company or not. Otherwise," she warned, "they turn up unannounced and surprise us, come hammering on the mind's door at 4 a.m. of a bad night and demand to know who deserted them, who betrayed them, who is going to make amends." Even if you think you are invisible they *will* find you and remind you who you no longer are—you're not all *that* obscure to the person you used to be.

The challenge is finding a way to be less obscure to yourself. If you could enter a different role equivalent to the one you used to play, the one in which you felt you had existence, you might become more apparent to yourself again. Your concentration on inhabiting

161

that new identity might keep you, as the old identity did, from wondering what underlies that external preoccupation. It's Riggan Thomson's goal in *Birdman.*

Many people—perhaps most?—undergo that alteration without ever experiencing a temporary sense of disappearance, made secure by the distractions of predictable routine, perhaps because "the center of thought and intention with which [they] normally identify" never let those exterior roles take precedence over their internal identity. Somehow, they never considered the roles they played as more than roles, never misidentified themselves as those external characters. If you have never been overwhelmed by that confusion, you are never obscure to yourself whatever change of roles you undergo; you can't fall into obscurity or imagine how anyone else could feel they had.

My sense of having fallen into obscurity and having disappeared has to do with my professional life and I try to remember how leaving their day jobs affected people in my family. My mother's father joined our local Civil Defense unit to serve as an occasional traffic control officer or security guard at special public events; my father worked on Soapbox Derby projects and received an award—a clock now on my bookcase, still ticking after nearly thirty years—as a Distinguished Lieutenant Governor with Optimist International. Neither defined himself by his paying job in the past, factory worker or salesman. Neither felt as if he had disappeared. Part of that sense of security about their identities likely grew not out of donning new roles but out of seeing those roles essentially as something outside their identities.

What I keep overlooking is that, in order to stew privately about my invisibility, I have to get out of the sightlines of family and acquaintances. Especially family. I'm still a husband, a father, a grandfather, an uncle, a sibling. What obscurity I may feel in any of those roles grows out of the independence of my wife, my children, my grandchildren, my nieces and nephews, my siblings. All are caught up in considering what to do with their own lives and, even as their interactions with me lessen and become less urgent than they sometimes have been, we still interact. I fall into obscurity with them all the time, as they do, in varying degrees, with me, their lives having become ever more complex and demanding. Sunday phonecalls and occasional visits keep us from being entirely invisible—keep us only moderately obscure—from one another, but we all still pay attention to one another.

Is all this simply an example of moving on, carrying on, progressing in the path that my grandparents and my parents took, that my children will take in emulation of their parents, that my grandchildren will one day take in emulation of their parents and grandparents?

Taking retirement—or being retired—is a predictable happenstance in our lives. It changes the direction in which we've been going, for the most part. It turns us into someone other than who we've seemed to be throughout our working lives. But, for most of us, our day jobs are not all there were to our days. They may have helped us ignore the passage of time by making every day almost the same, but time was still being measured by incremental alterations in the world around us, the world we lived in, the world within us. When you see someone every day—see yourself in the mirror every morning—you don't notice those alterations, until an old photo surfaces, an image from a yearbook, the sudden awareness that your grandchild is now taller than you or looks more like your son-in-law than he used to, and you are unable to divert your attention away from the obvious.

What I need to do is get out of the way of the person I've been all along and let him keep pursuing the passions—the innate desire for understanding, the need for expression—that he's evidenced all along; I need to let him connect to the core of the creature who has always existed. Every act of writing is an act of communication the writer performs with himself, even if he doesn't always interrogate it closely before he releases it into the world. It's a message to him from the person he actually is. Thinking what I think and being who I am hasn't changed with the change in my circumstances.

And the change in my circumstances hasn't made me obscure or invisible to my family, all those people who have always found me apparent, perceivable.

So perhaps I should feel content to be the kind of character who would write an essay like this, identify myself as someone doggedly reconciling himself to the circumstances of his actual existence, both physical and psychological. He might be able to keep doing this kind of thing, pursuing the questions that surface in his mind, trying to figure out how they came to be there and what they have to tell him. He might learn more about who has been there all along. He might slowly become more apparent to himself, more visible in a mirror. Sufficiently satisfied that he exists.

He might be able to get up all by himself.

POSTLUDE

Our children and their spouses, our grandchildren. They are most often a far-flung lot, resident on three different coasts. We treasure the moments when we can assemble them all in one place. It doesn't happen often.

All this while I've been looking over my shoulder at where I've come from, interrogating the past; these images remind me to look ahead and pay attention to the future. I don't think about the future—the distant future, that is—very much, but at the rate the weeks go by and the birthdays mount up, I'm more conscious of how limited my time in it is likely to be. When I look at these pictures now, it dawns on me that I am already their past and, in no time at all, will be ranked among their ancestors.

When we marry and have children, we stop being the end product of past mixed family lines and become a strand in future mixed family lines. My children are not only the offspring of a father and a mother but also the grandchildren of their parents' parents. If genetic material is distributed evenly, they are half my side of the family and half their mother's, but since I am not merely half Root, half Linderman, but actually quarter Root and quarter Ross and quarter Linderman and quarter Budnack, my children are one-eighth Root, one-eighth Ross, and so on, and their mother's half divides her parents' origins into quarters, makes our children four-eighths the families of her parents' parents. As it happens, my children's parents divorced and then married other divorcees with children, and those children were various proportions their parents' families and so on. In our present family my daughter and my wife's daughter

165

have both married and had wonderful children. Now everything we passed on to our children through our ancestral lines has been immediately halved in the genes of their children. The children all bear their fathers' last names for now—when the girls grow up they may marry and take their husbands' names or still keep their fathers' names or even revert to their mothers' names (this is the 21st Century, you know)—and the boys will be thought to carry on their fathers' lineages in books of genealogy. My son, the only boy of his generation in our family line, hasn't married or fathered children, and if we lived in a strict patriarchy, that would be cause for concern—he would automatically be heir to my condo and the aristocratic title that goes with it. But we don't.

In fact, the more I delve into genealogy and understand the complications of lineage, the more I wonder who they all are in that regard. It has nothing to do with my love and adoration for them all, the five adults, the five children, which is limitless, beyond measure. It has to do with individuality and my growing sense that, genetically, there are no individuals. Is individuality only an aspect of personality? But if I think that I can trace elements of my personality back to my parents and the prominent features of their personalities, and recognize that some elements of their personalities grew out of features of their parents' personalities, those Root-Ross and Linderman-Budnack identities, then I have to acknowledge that elements of our children's personalities have been influenced by features of their parents' personalities—who their mothers and their fathers were—and that our grandchildren will to some degree be molded by our children's personalities and their spouses' personalities and the families they all came from.

There are advantages and handicaps in what gets passed on from generation to generation. To know what's been passed on may require investigating the varied lineages that have led to each of them. What I've investigated here has only been part of my portion of their heritage. Our children and grandchildren have other lineages to trace if they would like a complete picture of who they are and where they come from. They'll have to decide for themselves what they really want to learn.

I wish them love and rewarding searches.

ACKNOWLEDGMENTS

Some portions of the book were first published, often in altered form, elsewhere:

"A Driving Lesson" as "The Driving Lesson," *Thread* 1:2 (Summer 2015).
Material in "Columnist" also appears in Betsy Root, *How to Develop Your Personality: The Buffalo* Courier-Express *Column April 5-August 14, 1937* (2012).
Material in "Interlude: Locks" is excerpted from "The Locks," *Ascent* (January 30, 2017).
"Some Mornings," *Contemporary Haibun Online* 14:3 (September 2018).
"Memory: A Triptych," *Lake Effect* 24 (Spring 2020).
"Mirrors," *Contemporary Haibun Online* 10:1 (April 2014).
"Rain," in "Beautiful Things," *River Teeth* (October 6, 2014).
"Wild and Precious," *Under the Sun* Issue 3 (June 24, 2015).
"A Perceivable Soul," in "Beautiful Things," *River Teeth* (May 20, 2019).

That this book appears in the world at all is through the generosity, energy, and thoughtfulness of Steven Harvey and Kathryn Winograd. Steve and Kathy were invaluable colleagues in a graduate school enterprise we shared in for nearly ten years—our students will remember those times fondly, I hope—and their editing of my writing for The Humble Essayist Press helped me feel ready to release this book into the world. The book and I have also benefitted from the kindness, wisdom, and tolerance of the families to which I am fortunately bound: Roots, Lindermans, Van Kirks, Prestons, Diszes, and Schauers in their multiple generations. Sue's love and patience continues to sustain me. I'm thankful for all these people.

WORKS CITED

Barnes, Julian. *Nothing to Be Frightened Of.* New York: Alfred A. Knopf, 2008.

Carroll, Lewis. *Alice in Wonderland.* 1865.

Cunningham, Michael. *The Snow Queen.* New York: Farrar, Straus and Giroux, 2014.

Detrick, Ronald P. *Great Is Thy Faithfulness: The Life and Times of Florence Elizabeth Root.* Wilmington: The Alpha-Omega Mission Press, 2000.

Didion, Joan. "On Keeping a Notebook," *Slouching Towards Bethlehem.* New York: Farrar, Straus, and Giroux, 1968.

Didion, Joan. *The Year of Magical Thinking.* New York: Alfred A. Knopf, 2005.

Hinton, David. *Hunger Mountain: A Field Guide to Mind and Landscape.* Boulder: Shambhala, 2012.

Huntington, Rev. E. B. *Genealogical Memoir of the Lo-Lathrop Family.* [N.P.] Mrs. Julia Huntington, 1884.

Iñárritu, Alejandro G., et al. *Birdman* or *(The Unexpected Virtue of Ignorance).* [Screenplay]

Makkai, Rebecca. *The Hundred-Year House.* New York: Viking, 2014.

McClanahan, Rebecca, *The Tribal Knot: A Memoir of Family, Community, and a Century of Change.* Bloomington: Indiana University Press, 2013.

Oliver, Mary. "The Summer Day," *House of Light.* Boston: Beacon Press, 1990.

Pride, Mike. "Donald Hall's Late Burst of Creativity," *The New Yorker.* October 13, 2018. <https://www.newyorker.com/books/page-turner/donald-halls-late-burst-of-creativity>

Root, Betsy. *How to Develop Your Personality: The Buffalo* Courier-Express *Column April 5-August 14, 1937.* Ed. Robert L. Root Jr. Glimmerglass Editions, 2012.

Root, James Pierce. *Root Genealogical Records 1600-1870.* New York: R. C. Root, Anthony & Co., 1870.

Simon, Paul. "Bookends," Simon & Garfunkel, *Bookends.* Columbia, 1968.

Simon, Paul. "Slip Slidin' Away," Paul Simon, *Still Crazy After All These Years.* Columbia, 1975.

Robert Root is the author of two essay collections, *Limited Sight Distance: Essays for Airwaves* and *Postscripts: Retrospections on Time and Place;* the memoir *Happenstance;* and the literary travel memoirs, *Recovering Ruth: A Biographer's Tale, Following Isabella: Travels in Colorado Then and Now,* and *Walking Home Ground: In the Footsteps of Muir, Leopold, and Derleth.* An Emeritus Professor of English at Central Michigan University, he also taught creative nonfiction in the low-residency MFA Program at Ashland University, the Lighthouse Writers Workshop, and the Loft Literary Center and has conducted nonfiction workshops in Alaska, Switzerland, and a number of American universities and conferences. He co-edited the anthology *The Fourth Genre: Contemporary Writers of/on Creative Nonfiction* and edited *Landscapes with Figures: The Nonfiction of Place.* He is also the author of *E. B. White: The Emergence of an Essayist, The Nonfictionist's Guide: On Reading and Writing Creative Nonfiction, Working at Writing: Columnists and Critics Composing,* and *Wordsmithery: A Guide to Working at Writing.* He has been an Artist-in-Residence at Isle Royale National Park, Rocky Mountain National Park, and Acadia National Park. His essays have been widely published and listed as Notable Essays in *Best American Essays.* His website is www.rootwriting.com. He lives in Wisconsin.

www.ingramcontent.com/pod-product-compliance
Lightning Source LLC
Chambersburg PA
CBHW031203270326
41931CB00006B/386